CHEDWORTH
LIFE IN A
ROMAN VILLA

SIMON ESMONDE CLEARY

in association with **National Trust**

Front cover illustration: A reconstruction of the villa from the
south-east, by Tony Kerins. (*National Trust*)
Back cover illustration: A section from the mosaic with scenes of
Dido and Aeneas from Vergil's *Aeneid*, at Low Ham villa, Somerset.
(*Taunton Museum*)

First published in association with the National Trust 2013

The History Press
The Mill, Brimscombe Port
Stroud, Gloucestershire, GL5 2QG
www.thehistorypress.co.uk

British Library Cataloguing in Publication Data.
A catalogue record for this book is available from the British Library.

ISBN 978 0 7524 8643 7

Typesetting and origination by The History Press
Printed and bound in Great Britain by
Marston Book Services Limited, Oxfordshire

CONTENTS

FOREWORD

BY TONY ROBINSON

This book is published to coincide with the completion of the multi-million-pound redevelopment of Chedworth Roman Villa. For anyone who has penetrated the depths of the Cotswolds and got to know the villa at Chedworth over the years, the transformation that has taken place recently is astonishing. From a much-loved little place in a sorry state, it has been transformed by the National Trust into one of the best archaeological sites to visit in Britain. A trip to Chedworth is no lonely stroll among mute walls and faded information panels, but now a journey into the exotic and surprising 'Golden Age' of Roman Britain.

The stories from Chedworth Roman Villa are fascinating, and not immediately obvious. When we think of Romans, our immediate thoughts are drawn to film and TV interpretations from *The Life of Brian* via *Gladiator* to *I Claudius*, *Rome* or even *Up Pompeii!*

Many of these ideas of ancient Rome and its empire relate to a different period, an earlier time, in the centuries either side of the birth of Christ. Chedworth flourished during the fourth century AD, some 300 years and many generations after the Roman invasion of Britain or the Rome of our collective imaginations. The fourth century AD was a different and more settled time in Roman Britain, which seems quite obvious once we think that 300 years ago from today, in the reign of Queen Anne, things were very different to how they now are, and we don't think of ourselves as being the same as people then.

By the fourth century even the poorest inhabitants in the Roman provinces of *Britannia* were aware they were citizens of an empire that was master of nearly all the known world. They were not a subjugated mass under an oppressive foreign yoke, but more an integral part of a Roman Empire that spread across much of the known world. Most inhabitants still led harsh and poor lives as peasant farmers, herdsmen, servants, labourers. But Roman society did allow some social mobility, through the army or through crafts and trade. Its long-established stability encouraged the arts, culture and religious diversity: so especially for the social elites, such as the owners of great villas like Chedworth, it was a 'Golden Age'.

Please visit Chedworth and experience this Golden Age for yourself. The stones are re-animated! Gone are the inadequate Victorian sheds which covered some of the remains but made it almost impossible to see anything. Suspended walkways allow us to walk the rooms as Romans, to see the full range of mod-cons, such as the luxurious underfloor heating. You can now see the mosaics in all their glory, including the whole length of the magnificent newly excavated 30m-long front gallery mosaic. And people have returned to the villa. You can watch a fine banquet in the grand dining room, the appetite whetted by spicy aromas and the sound of wine being poured. A trip to the bath house feels almost as hot and fuggy as it must have when the aromas of scented oils filled the air and the groans of sweating Romans echoed around.

This book by Simon Esmonde Cleary is a much needed and eloquent introduction to this fascinating period in history. The complete story of Chedworth is fully told, from the archaeological evidence to where Chedworth's place is in the wider Roman world. For anyone who is interested in archaeology, intrigued by Roman Britain, or has not even heard of the Golden Age, this book is for you.

INTRODUCTION

BY PETER SALWAY

For many of the general public who thought they knew something of the Romans, and of Roman Britain in particular, a visit to Chedworth Roman Villa contains a series of surprises. As Tony Robinson has pointed out in the Foreword, this is not the Rome of white togas, marble columns and soldiers resembling lobsters, of Julius Caesar, Augustus and Nero, of Christians and lions. Nor is it the Roman Britain of Claudius, Boudicca and Hadrian's Wall. Here the National Trust has chosen to concentrate for the visitor on the Late Roman period. In the context of Britain this roughly spans the fourth century AD with a few years on either side, with the villa at its height three centuries after the Roman Conquest. The Trust's decision is in spite of evidence for some Roman occupation on the site in the second and third centuries AD. The reason is because this is the time when the size and magnificence reached by the villa marks it out from all but a dozen or so other villas in Roman Britain and is the era to which its famous mosaics are assigned. It is a period little presented to the public in the UK, yet spectacularly full of colour and interest. It has frequently been described as the 'Golden Age' of Roman Britain. To historians of the wider Roman world – particularly medievalists – it is often seen as the first phase of the Byzantine Empire, starting from the founding of Constantinople in AD 324 or the legalisation of Christianity in 312 by the first Christian emperor, Constantine the Great.

Indeed, a fundamental difference between the fourth century and earlier times is that religion was now a dominating issue in politics, and the conflicts between Christianity as promoted by almost every emperor and the traditional faiths of gods and goddesses – and between differing interpretations of Christianity itself – were centre stage. Persecuted viciously at the beginning of the century, by the end Christians saw the practice of the traditional religions outlawed, even in the home, and the sad history of the suppression of Christian heresies by the State was beginning. Chedworth is one of the few places in Britain where it is possible to detect echoes of those religious conflicts. Nor is this the only aspect in which the villa takes its place in the context of the wider late Roman world. In 1995 the archaeologist Simon Ellis wrote that 'by the late Empire the British elite had deepened their understanding of classical culture to the extent of adopting complex social behaviour and symbolic expression that would not have been out of place in the residences of the chief citizens of the Empire'.

I entirely concur with Simon Esmonde Cleary in accepting this opinion as it is the best fit with the archaeological evidence, but it is important to note that it does not meet with universal assent. There is quite a strong current of opinion that likes to see Britain as resistant to Roman culture, and explores features previously regarded as revealing 'Romanisation' to identify specifically 'regional' or 'British' variations. This partly comes out of a welcome trend towards studying regional differences – whether as regards different provinces of the empire or parts of Roman Britain itself – and differences between the various sectors within the population itself, and at different points in time. There seem, however, to be other less-helpful threads running through some of the current attitudes among archaeologists.

One of these is an attempt to see Britain under Roman rule as an evanescent phase of foreign occupation that had little effect on a native Britishness, temporarily interrupting a claimed 'natural trajectory' of the islands' culture. A second (not always separated from this) is characterised every so often by presenters of TV programmes declaring 'I don't much like the Romans'. Behind that, I suspect, are feelings hostile to aggressive militarist societies and sympathetic to the prevailing mood of anti-colonialism. Admirable though these sentiments may be, they are distractingly anachronistic when applied to Roman Britain, especially to the Late Roman period. There is a fundamental difference from the empires of European states in modern times. Like them, the Roman Empire started as a power ruling conquered peoples. Unlike them it evolved – largely by accident – by absorbing the conquered into a single state. Indeed, from the end of the first century, most emperors themselves came from the provinces, from the early third there was a single common citizenship, and from then on one could say that effectively the provinces had taken over the centre. Ironically, the modern anti-colonialist feelings are the mirror image of what Victorian British themselves thought about the Roman Empire and their own. While it may be fair to see Britain in the first century as conquered and occupied, by the fourth more or less every permanent resident within the Roman frontiers who was not a slave was a Roman citizen. Differences now were not between citizen and the rest but of an increasingly polarised and formalised class system.

Another school of thought insists on using archaeology alone and rejecting the classical literary sources. This is claimed to be more 'scientific', on the grounds that the ancient authors had their own agendas, were writing from a Roman perspective, and also tended to use *topoi* (set-piece standard phrases and passages used, for example, in describing battles). This school of thought also points out that most of the writing is not specifically about Britain and is almost all by persons not known to have first-hand experience of the British Isles. However, to ignore the ancient authors is as sensible as for a doctor to ignore what the patients themselves say. They may have all sorts of reasons for not describing their symptoms accurately, but their words are themselves evidence towards a diagnosis.

By combining the literary evidence with the archaeology we can begin to see how a great house like Chedworth worked. In order to provide hospitality – an activity of great significance in how the members of the elite related to one another – the villa-owner required certain categories of space: somewhere to receive the visitors, somewhere to entertain them (if they were of the rank where entertainment was expected) and somewhere to accommodate them, their companions and servants. It was also an integral part of the process to endeavour impress them with the status, wealth and taste of the host. The fourth century could, in the words of Simon Esmonde Cleary 'do magnificence'. One of the more frustrating features is that we know nothing about the identity of the owner of the villa. Even what sort of person he or she might have been is less certain than has commonly been stated. For many years the prime objective at Chedworth and other Roman villas open to the public in Britain has been to disabuse the visitor of the idea that the residents were Italians. This has meant emphasizing that the most likely owners were members of the local gentry, descendants of the pre-Roman British elite of the local tribe (the Dobunni) who had adopted Roman ways. This is certainly quite likely of the first owners of the land and perhaps of its occupiers for several generations. However the changes in government and society in the late

Roman period included a shift in power and prestige from local government to central. Roman Britain, originally one province, was subdivided into four (eventually five), command of the armed forces on the island was separated off from the civil government, and the provincial governors were brought under two new higher levels of administration, sited respectively in London and Trier, in modern Germany. The 'small government' of the early empire that had depended on willing local gentry was replaced by the 'big government' of centrally appointed officials. This will inevitably have brought substantial numbers of government appointees to the new provincial capitals such as Cirencester – the second-largest walled city in Britain – and means that we cannot any longer automatically assume local owners. If they *were* local gentry their world had changed. Membership of the local council had once been keenly contested, with leading local families vying with one another to gain office and prestige through benefactions and sponsorships, often for public buildings or entertainments. Early in the fourth century, however, Constantine had appropriated the funds of the local authorities, and the individual councillors were made responsible for collecting taxes, making up from their own private assets any shortfalls. Understandably, local office was now avoided, and gentry used many devices to become ineligible. Soldiers and Christian clergy, for example, were exempt, as were holders of certain formal ranks in civil society, obtained either through a term of office in certain qualifying public posts or by imperial favour, in some cases requiring particular levels of personal wealth. The local gentry's interest now, therefore, lay in joining the official and social circles of the imperial administration, chiefly centred on the provincial governor.

The owners at Chedworth – particularly of the extended villa – may not however have been locals at all. We know that some of the super-rich in the empire, operating at an oligarchic level of personal wealth, had many properties, including one – a woman – with estates in Italy, Spain, the North African provinces and Britain. There were many others in more modest but still substantial affluence with more than one villa. We therefore have to allow for non-local owners – including absentee landlords – who might be from anywhere in the Roman world, with the possibility that the host at the villa might be a tenant, whose background and ethnicity could be equally diverse.

Integral to the running of a villa were the servants, and there is evidence that that the greater the number the more it added to the owner's prestige. Servants in big houses in our period seem to have had specialist functions. Kitchen porters, for example, brought the food up from the kitchen and handed it over to the staff stationed in the dining-room. The latter themselves had specialised functions – carrying the food inside the room, serving wine or washing the guests' hands and feet. The servants had a pecking-order between them, and it was possible to be promoted up the chain, starting with juveniles occupying the most junior positions.

Were the domestic staff slaves? The common conception of slavery in the Roman world is heavily coloured by *Spartacus* and *Gladiator* and knowledge of black slavery in the New World. In reality it was much more complex, and we cannot assume that all servants were slaves. Enormous numbers of slaves had appalling lives, but some, depending on their masters, held remarkably powerful positions. Nor was slavery necessarily for life. There was considerable social mobility. Some bought their freedom, others were freed by their masters. Freedmen ran large areas of administration, and in a great household were regularly men of business or the estate manager, with their freedwomen wives acting as housekeeper. Their children were automatically full Roman citizens. Outside the household some slaves may have worked on the estate, but it is likely that many of the supplies and services for the villa were provided by tenants (*coloni*), nominally free but now tied to their occupation by law, in the fourth century a recent innovation due to acute shortage of agricultural labour.

The identification of Chedworth villa as a grand private house is generally accepted, but it is important to note two other interpretations that are favoured by some reputable archaeologists. They are incompatible with one another. One is that it was certainly a residential villa but revealing joint ownership by two or more proprietors. Essentially this hypothesis – known as the Unit-System theory – is based on the identification of duplicated sets of rooms, and is argued to reflect a system of society surviving in Britain and Gaul even among the elite that differed from that general in the classical world. It implies that the apparently Roman form of British villas conceals a deliberate adoption of the external appearance and interior equipment such as mosaics and hypocausts but with a reordering of the disposition of space to suit local social structures based around multiple family units. The author of the present book, however, is convinced (I think correctly) that Chedworth is much more easily interpreted in the context of the social usages of the Late Roman world at large.

The other theory that has had respectable support proposes that Chedworth was not a residential villa but a hostel for pilgrims visiting the nearby temple discovered by the River Coln to the south-east. It was certainly a very substantial structure, with a massive base or podium constructed in huge blocks of fine masonry, each 4 x 2ft, and columns around 12ft tall. Its design remains uncertain, and it is just possible that it was a mausoleum rather than a temple. The principal arguments for the 'pilgrimage centre' theory are based on the absence so far from the villa of agricultural-estate buildings, the multiplicity of relatively small rooms, and the discovery of various objects of a religious nature, such as the altar from the *nymphaeum*. There is, however, a fatal flaw in the argument. The excavation in the 1920s was extremely badly reported: all that one can say is that there is no evidence for activity at the temple beyond around AD 275 at the latest. Yet at the villa the expansion that produced the multiplicity of rooms did not begin before 275 at the earliest. In the absence of further excavations, the hostel theory has to be shelved.

The question of how and when this villa was abandoned and the nature of its 'afterlife' is examined later in the book. But whatever the context it was not 'what every schoolboy knows' – that in 410 'the Romans left Britain'. We have already noted that for 200 years all the free inhabitants of the provinces had been Roman citizens, and sudden emigration of the entire population is unimaginable – and quite contrary to what evidence remains. What we can say is that by 410 the central Roman government had lost control of Britain, but there was no reason for anyone to think it would not eventually be resumed. After all, it had been the everyday fact of life for perhaps a dozen generations. It is true that in the previous year the provincials had expelled the imperial officials from their posts, but this was no independence movement: the officials were those of a usurper, not of the legitimate emperor. The former seems to have removed the bulk of the remaining garrison from Britain, while the latter was unable to regain control – either now or later – due to acute problems on the Continent and his own considerable incompetence.

We may suspect from the archaeology that the villa ceased to operate as a great house some time before these events, but without an emperor to provide the legal authority for the whole administrative system or the ultimate enforcement of the everyday civil and criminal law on which the economic and political system depended it is inconceivable that the life of a great house like Chedworth could have continued unchanged. If the locals assumed that ordinary life would eventually return, their expectations were never fulfilled. It was over 1,000 years before unfortified great houses appeared again in the English countryside.

ONE

SETTING THE SCENE

'The discovery of the Roman villa in these woods originated with an under gamekeeper, engaged in ferreting rabbits, and was first brought under my notice in June 1864.' This is the account that has passed into history, legend almost, the 'ferret and Farrer' story. It was penned by the man responsible for uncovering the villa, James Farrer MP, uncle of and guardian to the 3rd Lord Eldon, owner of the Stowell estate within which the site lay. It was Farrer who not only had the villa disinterred but also had its remains preserved above ground and had a museum built on the site to display the more notable finds made in bringing the villa to light (see colour plate 1). These decisions were to make Chedworth one of the most significant and famous villas to come down to us from the Roman period in Britain, since even today so few of the many hundreds that once existed are visible above ground. In 1924 the site passed to the National Trust, and it is thanks to the Trust's efforts that in 2011 the impressive new building that covers the western range of the villa was constructed, made possible by generous funding from the Heritage Lottery Fund. As part of its core mission, the National Trust seeks to help its members, visitors, and other people with an interest in its properties to understand the significance of these places to the people who lived and worked in them, and how what we see today was shaped by the attitudes and values of people in the past. That is what this book hopes to do – to provide a readable explanation of the Chedworth Roman villa, with more space than is available in the necessarily rather summary presentation of the villa in the guidebook for use on site. It draws on the detailed and specialist knowledge that will appear in the academic monograph that will formally publish the villa, and also wider knowledge about late Roman villas in Britain and beyond, and seeks to make these results accessible to a wider readership.

The aim is that this book should enable someone who has visited the site and wants to know more about it to be able to do so and to see how our knowledge and understanding of it has been built up. Equally, it aims to allow someone who has not visited the site, but perhaps intends to, to learn about it in advance. It can also act as an introduction more generally to life in a villa in Roman Britain; why it was laid out the way it was, why it was equipped with its remarkable range of mosaics, who lived in it and what their place in the history and culture of (Roman) Britain was. The stout-hearted can read it through from cover to cover, but it is also designed to be dipped into in order to find out about particular aspects of life at Roman Chedworth, which should be signalled by the chapter titles or found through the index.

The bulk of the rest of the book will relate to the villa in its fully developed form in its most prosperous and splendid period in the middle of the fourth century AD. This period does not come out of nowhere: the mid-fourth-century phase is the culmination of a long history of development. This initial chapter is intended to set the scene, to look at the natural features of the site of the villa and to look at what we know of the early development of the complex of buildings leading up to the emergence of the fully fledged villa of the fourth century.

GEOLOGY & NATURAL RESOURCES

The Roman villa was built in a small, steep-sided valley or combe running east–west and opening at its eastern end into the valley of the River Coln. The geology of the area is dominated by the limestones of the Cotswolds, here in particular the Inferior Oolites (oolite, from *oon*, the Greek for egg, refers to the distinctive granular texture of the limestones of much of the Cotswolds). Like all the Cotswolds area, these bands of stone slope from north-west to south-east. The underlying geology of the Chedworth combe is limestone of the Aston Formation (a subdivision of the Inferior Oolite), with the overlying Birdlip and Salperton Formations present at the east end of the valley and to the west of the valley respectively. Interleaved with the limestones are beds of Fullers Earth, a fine clay that was an important influence on human settlement in the valley of the villa. Whereas the limestones are permeable to water, which will drain down through them, the Fullers Earth, being clay, is impermeable. The water therefore has to lie on top of the Fullers Earth, forming a 'perched water-table', a body of water that does not drain downwards into a river or stream and its associated water-table. Due to the north-west to south-east trend of the Cotswolds, the water perched on the Fullers Earth will tend to flow south-eastwards, sometimes encountering a valley or other feature where it comes to the surface as a spring or spring-line. This is what happens in the Chedworth combe, where water perched on the Fullers Earth breaks out of the northern side, most notably in the north-western corner of the valley, where it forms a perennial spring, a permanent source of drinkable water, later captured by the Romans in the *nymphaeum* of the villa.

With the retreat of the glaciers of the last Ice Age some 10,000 and more years ago, the countryside of Britain became largely wooded. One of the earliest and most profound environmental changes caused by humans in these islands was the gradual deforestation of the landscape of Britain from about 5,000 years ago in order to turn it over to growing crops and raising livestock. With the consequent loss of the tree canopy to intercept rain and the root-mat to stabilise soil, this led to massive soil erosion from valley sides down into valley bottoms and rivers. We have no direct evidence for this from the

1. Nineteenth-century engraving of the *nymphaeum*. (*British Library*)

Chedworth combe yet, due to the lack of appropriate excavation and analyses, but it is overwhelmingly probable that this involved the combe also. With the loss of the tree cover, over time erosion of the slopes of the combe would have produced fine-grained earths and clays that tended to migrate downslope and are often found in archaeological excavation, and have probably infilled the bottom of the valley to some depth.

The present appearance of the combe may be misleading, particularly in comparison with its appearance in the Roman period. Currently the slopes and top of the combe are clothed with trees, but this is a reflection of the current needs of the Stowell estate, whose lands surround the National Trust's property containing the Roman villa. In the Roman period it is possible, indeed probable (see p. 124), that the slopes and ridges were bare of trees or that there were many fewer trees than now. By the late centuries BC the Cotswold landscape was probably largely open and farmed, rather as it is today, with tree cover very restricted but nonetheless an important economic resource, as we shall see in Chapter 6. One other natural feature to note that may have influenced human use of the valley is that in the depths of winter, from late November to late March, the combe spends much of the day in shade, with the sun only clearing the ridge-tops to the south and west in the middle of the day. Combined with the natural propensity of cold air to sink, this makes the combe something of a 'frost-hollow' and in periods of prolonged subzero temperatures, with or without snow, a pretty inhospitable place. This could have meant that human activity, even in the Roman period, was seasonal, with a preference for occupation in spring, summer and autumn.

THE 'EARLY VILLA'

It is from the late prehistoric period during the Iron Age, in the fourth century BC, that we have our first direct evidence for human activity in the valley. Excavations in 2001 in the lower garden of the site encountered the burial of a child aged about one year at death; it was placed lying on its right side in the crouched position common at this period. A radiocarbon assay of the bones gave a date centring on 350 BC, and just to the north of the burial was a sherd of middle Iron Age pottery, of the same general date. Clearly, therefore, there was some form of human use of or settlement in the valley, but without further evidence of the same date the child burial remains a pointer but no more. The next period for which we have evidence is, of course, the Roman, stretching from the invasion of these islands under the Emperor Claudius in AD 43 for some 400 years, until the collapse of the western part of the Roman Empire, along with the loss of Roman Britain in the early part of the fifth century (from here on all dates will be AD unless otherwise stated). As noted above, the bulk of this book will be concerned with the villa in its heyday, around the middle of the fourth century, but equally there is clear evidence both from the structural history of the site and from finds of coins and pottery that this was just the culmination of a history of development from simpler beginnings, beginnings that we now need to try to understand as best we can.

This is no easy task; the nineteenth-century uncovering of the villa, to which we owe the great majority of what is visible today, was more concerned with the recovery of a two-dimensional plan of the villa, along with mosaics, hypocausts and so on, than with trying to understand the chronological sequence of events on the site. Nevertheless, even as early as Farrer's work in 1864 and his published summary of it in 1865 (see p. 168), it was recognised that there were parts of the complex that were earlier than the fully developed villa of the fourth century. Like Farrer, we can identify portions of the site that antedated the main phase, but what we cannot as yet do is give them either a *relative* chronology, i.e. which part was built first and which parts were later, and in what order; or an *absolute* chronology, i.e. dates in calendar years.

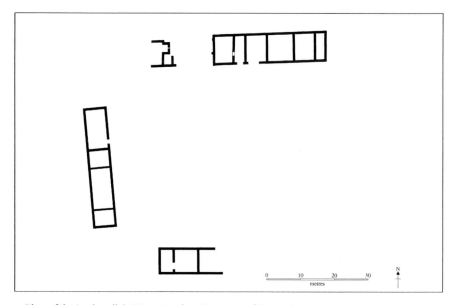

2. Plan of the 'early villa'. (*Henry Buglass / University of Birmingham*)

The evidence that there was this earlier phase (or phases) is structural; when a new building was constructed up against an existing one, the walls were not bonded together, rather the new one was butted up against the earlier structure, leaving a 'straight' or 'butt' joint in the masonry, where one can see which building was constructed first. This is the main structural evidence we have for the so-called 'early villa' phase(s), though there is some other, supplementary evidence that will be noted.

We shall start with the west range, which seems in the fully developed villa to have been essentially suites of reception rooms. The original southern end of this range was the wall which currently divides the main part of Room 5 from the smaller, southern part. This southern part is clearly an addition and involved the demolition of most of the original southern wall of Room 5. South again of the extension to Room 5, the southernmost room of the west range, Room 5a, was itself a further addition. At the northern end, the hypocaust furnaces for the baths, Room 16, are likewise an addition, so the original north wall of this range was the north wall of what became the bath suite, terminating Rooms 12 and 15 on their northern sides. The subsequent re-buildings (such as the creation of the bath suite at the northern end of the range), re-floorings (such as the insertion of the hypocausts and mosaics in Rooms 5, 5a and 6) and reuses (of Rooms 7 and 8) mean that all trace of the original floorings and uses of the rooms in this range have been lost.

In the north wing, it is clear that the central block of rooms, Rooms 26 to 29a, are earlier than the rooms to either side of them. On the western side, the construction of Room 25 put out of use the original stokehole to Room 26 which had been through its west wall; there is also a butt joint between the south wall of Room 25 and the west wall of Room 26. On the eastern side, the north and south walls of Room 30 butt up against the east wall of Room 29a; in addition, the front (south) wall of the range fronting onto the gallery is slightly inset from the line of the south wall of Rooms 26 to 29a; also, the south wall of the gallery has a butt joint with the existing gallery wall. As with the west range it is not possible to say how this earlier building was used, since the nineteenth-century excavations did not penetrate sufficiently far down to uncover floors of this phase or phases. Nevertheless, the evidence we have suggests that the pattern of rooms in this part of the north wing was created in the 'early villa' phase by the building of the partition walls and persisted through into the fully developed villa.

In the south wing, it is again clear from the butt joints that what is now the west wall of Room 1b was originally the western gable wall of another free-standing building, comprising at least Rooms 1b, 1 and 1a, possibly with further unexcavated rooms to the east. Again, we do not know what the original uses of this building were. Excavations by Sir Ian Richmond in the early 1960s (see p. 185) showed that the west wall of Room 1b had originally carried a timber-framed upper part; this had burnt down leaving the mark produced by the burning of the horizontal sill beam laid along the top of the stonework. When the wall was rebuilt, the passage of the builders left a layer of mud sandwiched between the top of the original wall and the bottom of the new build.

The structural evidence, therefore, shows us that prior to the 'great rebuilding' of the turn of the third and fourth centuries, the head of the combe was occupied by three buildings, each built of stone, at least in their lower parts, and consisting of a single line of rooms. We do not know in what order they were built, or whether they were all in use at the same time. The latter is strongly suggested by the fact that all three were incorporated into the fully developed villa, so must have been in existence, even if possibly not all then in use. But whether they were all built at the same time or whether one was the first to be built with the other two added later is currently impossible to tell. Clearly they exercised a determining effect on the fully developed villa since they established the location and orientation of its main wings, including the way in which the west range is at an angle to the other two wings.

We do not know, either, at what date these buildings were constructed. Our best evidence comes from the layer of mud trampled over the west wall of the southern building when it was rebuilt after the fire; this contained a number of sherds of pottery of types current in the mid-second century. This suggests that the south building at least was probably constructed in the first half of the second century. As well as the structural evidence for earlier buildings, there is also the evidence of coins and pottery. The bulk of the coins recovered from the villa (see p. 137) date to the later third and fourth centuries, but there is a body of second-century coins, mostly of large copper-alloy denominations, such as the *as* and the *sestertius*, but also some silver *denarii*. Now while an individual second-century coin might exceptionally survive into the fourth century, it is next to impossible to see a group of them, as at Chedworth, surviving in this way. Therefore, such a group must argue for occupation and use of the site in the second century, probably also into the first half of the third century when hardly any new coins were supplied and later second-century issues continued to circulate.

The same is true of the pottery: as well as fourth-century pieces, there is a body of pottery datable to the second century, in particular the glossy red pottery, sometimes with moulded surface decoration, which we call samian ware, made in central Gaul in the region around modern Clermont-Ferrand. There are more local products which can also be dated to the second and on into the third centuries. The conclusion must be that some or all of the three 'early villa' buildings were occupied in the course of the second century, and quite probably constructed then. Whether there were any structures on the site from even earlier in the Roman period in the first century, possibly constructed in timber, we simply do not know; neither do we know whether the Roman-period structures were a new development or whether they succeeded late Iron Age occupation in the combe from before the Roman invasion of 43. One piece of evidence that there could have been timber buildings in the combe was recovered in the 2001 excavations in the lower garden, where alongside a metalled trackway there were found two holes to hold upright posts. These post-holes probably formed part of a timber structure flanking the trackway and probably dated to the second century.

The buildings of the 'early villa' phase were incorporated into the 'great rebuilding' of the villa somewhere around the turn of the third and fourth centuries (again the dating evidence is not conclusive). To accomplish this, the three galleries were built fronting the three wings, connecting them up and providing a uniform visual appearance. The cross-gallery was constructed to enclose the garden court and to demarcate it from the lower, outer court-yard. Projecting from the middle of the length of the south-wing gallery,

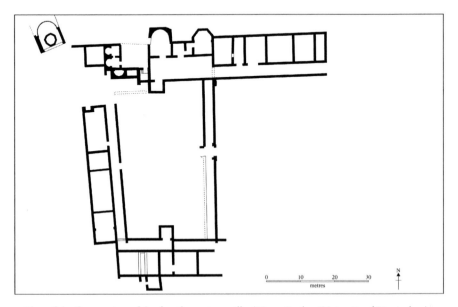

3. Plan of the first version of the fourth-century villa. (*Henry Buglass/University of Birmingham*)

facing onto the garden court, was Room 2, with a matching structure in the north wing. The existing 'early villa' buildings were then extended and joined up behind the galleries, to present a unified appearance, broken only at the north-western angle with the prospect up to the *nymphaeum*, the water shrine where the spring came out of the valley side. Whether all these extensions, particularly the two in the north wing, were undertaken at the same time we cannot as yet know, though it is clear that the eastern extension to the north wing was later than the 'great rebuilding' since its gallery is joined onto and therefore later than the gallery fronting the central part of the wing. At this time, if not earlier, the south wing was prolonged eastwards to balance the north wing. In this way was created the elaborate, integrated complex which filled the combe and used its slopes, and which will be the focus of the next five chapters.

TWO

THE LAYOUT OF THE LATE ROMAN VILLA

This chapter will contain the naming of parts. It will look at the evidence we have for the layout of the villa in the fourth century, particularly the mid- to later fourth century, which is the period for which we have the most evidence and which is the period of the remains on view to the public today. It will take the form of a tour of the villa, starting with the west range, which from its position at the end of the main axis of the villa was clearly an important part of the whole complex – this is reflected in the lavishness of the mosaics in the range. The north wing will come next, partly because it shares some of the characteristics of the west range in having a bath suite and a number of mosaics, but also because, like the west range, we have its more or less complete plan. The south wing will be considered last because we know much less about it, and also because it seems to have served rather different purposes to the other two. For each wing the main groups of rooms (such as bathhouses) will be identified and what we know of each room's function(s) and history outlined. Therefore, the chapter will lay out what we know, or think we know, about the development and use of the main phase of the villa in the fourth century. Some of this description will on occasion be fairly technical. If persevered with, it will give a good grounding in the evidence from which discussions in the subsequent chapters take their points of departure. On the other hand, the discussions in these other chapters are written so that the more detailed evidence presented in this chapter is not crucial to understanding them; so this chapter is a useful but not an indispensable prelude to the later chapters.

A few words need to be said about the limits to our knowledge as a result of the older excavations. For all the work that was carried out in the 100 years or so since the initial discovery of the villa in 1864, we have very little surviving information. The Victorian excavators did not appreciate the importance of keeping detailed records of what they found where; they were what we would now call 'antiquaries' interested in uncovering a Roman villa rather than archaeologists concerned with the detailed recording of a site and its finds in order to understand it. There are, therefore, no detailed records. Neither is there any detailed publication of what they had found, only short notices in local newspapers and in some of the local and national archaeological journals that were then coming into being and which would in due course come to be published annually. So we only have an outline account of the buildings and some mentions of the more notable finds within them. In this, they were of their time and it would be pointless and unfair to criticise them; doubtless in 150 years some of what we do (and do not do) will likewise seem hopelessly primitive.

Much the same can be said of further work on the villa and of the programmes of consolidation and management of the remains through the first half of the twentieth century. Even the excavations by Sir Ian Richmond in the late 1950s and '60s leave a lot to be desired since whatever records he kept have not survived. One of the problems this leaves us with is that sometimes we cannot be sure if a feature recorded in a room was there from the beginning or was the result of a later alteration. For instance, in the part of the north wing which originated in the 'early villa', and thus was occupied for two centuries and more, some of the rooms have fittings such as ovens (e.g. Room 31); we cannot be sure when they were constructed, at the beginning or later on, so the room may have changed its function. It is necessary to be aware of these problems in order to understand the many places where we do not know what the exact state of affairs in the Roman period was. However, without the work of the Victorian and later excavators we would not have the Chedworth villa at all.

The remains of the walls excavated, if left open and unconsolidated, would soon have fallen apart as frost and thaw forced the stone and the mortar to expand and contract and gradually to disintegrate. From the time of Lord Eldon onwards there have been programmes of consolidation of the walls and of protection of their tops, for instance with the little caps using Roman roof slates. The problem for us is that though these works generally used Roman stonework from the rubble of the villa, and thus are in keeping with the Roman structures, no record was kept of the actual Roman stonework and the walls were either almost completely rebuilt or had a new facing applied to the surviving Roman core. The result is that almost all the walls we see at Chedworth today are, in fact, nineteenth- or twentieth-century reconstructions. Though they give a good idea of where the Roman walls ran, they mean that important information about the original walls is lost. In particular, this involves the order of construction of the various walls.

When we can examine the original fabric, it is usually possible to work out which walls are of the same build (contemporary) and which are later additions. This is because walls built at the same time will normally use the same sort of stone, the same mortar, and the construction of the different walls will be integral. Where there are later walls, one can see different types or sizes of stone or a different mortar mix and so they can be told apart from the earlier versions. Crucially, where later walls met existing walls the builders rarely went to the effort of dismantling part of the existing wall to key the new one in. At Chedworth the modern consolidation and rebuilding has often masked this sort of evidence which is critical for working out the sequence of the complex, so we remain uncertain over many details of what happened and in what order. Another effect of the modern rebuilding is that it may have masked where there were originally doorways. Sometimes this seems to leave no way into a room (for instance, some of the rooms in the north wing) or it has obscured connecting doorways. This makes it difficult to reconstruct the patterns of circulation in the Roman period: which areas interconnected and which areas had no access to each other. Finally, it is clear that most of the pottery, metalwork and other finds from the first 100 years or so of work on the villa were disposed of, with only some of the finer pieces being retained; moreover, there is no record of where the great majority of material was found. Huge amounts of potential information about the dating and use of the villa have simply disappeared.

With these caveats in mind, let us turn to the excavated remains of the villa plan and to what these may tell us about the ways in which the various parts of the complex developed in the fourth century. Overall, the plan of the villa is very easy to grasp: an elongated U-shape, with long, parallel north and south wings which run north-north-west to south-south-east and a shorter west range at a slight angle to the other two, more truly aligned north–south. The alignments of the north and and south wings and the west range had been fixed by the pre-existing buildings of the 'early villa' discussed in the previous chapter.

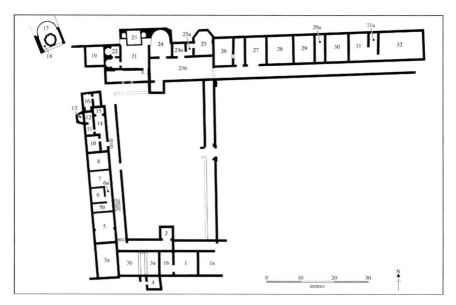

4. Plan of the entire fourth-century villa. (*Henry Buglass/University of Birmingham*)

The western third or so of the fourth-century villa was partitioned off by a cross-gallery with gatehouse; this division was reinforced by its also creating two different levels. The western third, beyond the cross-gallery, lay around what we call the 'inner courtyard', at a higher level than the area to the east, the 'outer courtyard'. The part of the north wing to the east of the cross-gallery and thus fronting onto the outer courtyard was artificially raised to maintain the higher level of the inner courtyard; there seems to have been no direct access to this from the outer courtyard so it needs to be thought of as a prolongation of the inner courtyard. By chance, what is now visible of the villa is the inner courtyard element, the north wing, the west range and the part of the south wing west of the cross-gallery. In essence, the plan of the inner courtyard shows simple, long galleries off which opened ranges of rooms, with rare exceptions no more than one room deep.

One final point: many of the rooms in the villa were given numbers by early workers, particularly in the 1960s. These have been used on all subsequent plans and in all subsequent discussions and presentations of the villa and are used in the present display of the site. They will therefore be retained here, even though there are problems, particularly in that some rooms and spaces do not have an assigned number.

THE GALLERIES

First of all, a consideration of the galleries, the long connecting spaces fronting the rooms in each of the three wings. Such spaces have often been referred to as 'corridors', but the word 'galleries' has been preferred here because of its connotations. A corridor essentially signifies a means of getting from one part of a building to another; by contrast, a gallery evokes the 'long galleries' in Tudor and Jacobean great houses that were not simply to do with getting from A to B, but were in themselves important spaces in which the wealth of the owner was displayed and in which people congregated and interacted. While not meaning to say that the 'galleries' at Chedworth villa performed exactly the same functions as the later ones, it does allow us to think of them as more than just spaces to walk along; more like places where people might meet and socialise.

The fact that the galleries fronting the west and north wings had mosaic floors like reception rooms or the baths supports the idea that they were important spaces rather than just functional passageways. It is also worth noting a modern view of these galleries that is almost certainly wrong, certainly for Chedworth. Many modern reconstruction drawings and paintings of Romano-British villas, including the ones of Chedworth, show these galleries as open, fronted by colonnades, the pillars sometimes on low dwarf walls.

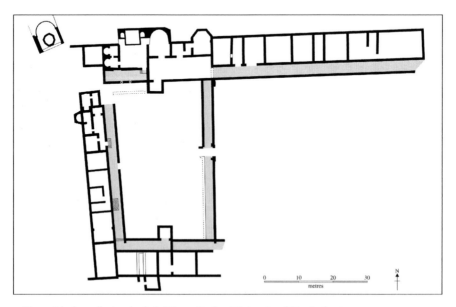

5. Plan with the galleries shaded. (*Henry Buglass/University of Birmingham*)

Indeed, the columns found at Chedworth and re-erected next to the north baths may themselves have been partly responsible for this vision of villas. In fact, it is unlikely that this system of colonnades was used: at Chedworth it cannot have been. The reason is simple: climate. An open colonnade at Chedworth, where the north and west galleries were floored with mosaics, would have let in the rain, soaking the mosaics. In itself this would have been bad for them and would have encouraged the growth of mould and moss. In winter it would have been disastrous as frost would have attacked the mosaics, with differential expansion of the tesserae and mortar forcing them to expand and move the only way available to them, upwards, causing them to heave and start disintegrating (this in fact happened to the dining-room mosaics in the 1940s). This would have been a real risk for the Chedworth villa, where the valley is a frost-hollow. Therefore, rather than some quasi-Mediterranean colonnade, we should imagine instead solid walls pierced by windows that could be closed against bad weather.

One other feature of the north and south galleries deserves mention. Halfway along each there is a space projecting out from the line of the gallery into the inner courtyard (that in the south wing is Room 2; that in the north wing has no number). Clearly designed to be symmetrical and to articulate the facades of the galleries (the entrance in the west range gallery would have performed a similar function there), how they were used is unclear. They could have been elaborate entrances or porches; they could have been bays in which to sit and look out onto the inner courtyard. On the Continent and sometimes in Britain such structures were placed in axis with important rooms such as the dining room as part of a contrived vista out across a gallery through the projecting chamber into the open space beyond. For the north wing this might hold good, since the projecting space is opposite the apsidal Room 24 (see below). For the south wing it is more problematic since the wing in general seems not to be of high status and the projecting Room 2 is across the gallery from the otherwise unremarkable Room 1b; it may be that the desire for symmetry was the deciding factor.

Before leaving the galleries it is worth considering the cross-gallery. Clearly its role was to act as the screen that closed off the inner courtyard and its buildings from the outer courtyard and to control access to the inner courtyard through its gateway. But it may also have served a distributive function, channelling certain types of visitor. Unfortunately, we do not know whether the northern and southern ends of the gallery communicated directly with the north- and south-wing galleries; modern reconstruction has obscured this. If they did, then the southern part of the cross-gallery could have taken people directly from the gatehouse to the southern service wing without them penetrating into the inner courtyard. Likewise, the northern part could have taken people directly to the vestibule to the important apsidal Rooms 24 and 25, to which we shall return later, again without them being allowed to go further into the inner courtyard and its buildings. The form of the cross-gallery is unknown. As just argued, it might very well have been enclosed, with just windows for lighting; but as there seem to have been no mosaics one could also envisage it as a sort of loggia with the eastern side colonnaded and therefore looking down on the lower courtyard and out beyond to the open countryside. It should be noted that the mis-alignment now visible in the southern part of the eastern wall of the cross-gallery is probably due to faulty modern reconstruction rather than an original feature.

THE WEST RANGE

The west range lay at the end of the main axis of the villa and was the range that directly faced the person entering through the cross-gallery gatehouse. From its siting it was clearly one of the most important components of the entire Chedworth complex. It originated in the 'early villa' phase, comprising from the main part of Room 5 along to Room 15. In the 'great rebuilding' at the turn of the third and fourth centuries it was extended to the south by the addition of the extension to Room 5 and the construction of Room 5a, and the gallery was added along its eastern face. The uncovering of the gallery mosaic showed that under the modern rebuilding of the walls two or three courses of original Roman masonry survived. It was clear that near the southern end of the gallery there was originally a doorway through into Room 5 and the mosaic continued under the later blocking of the doorway. This shows that at the time of the 'great rebuilding' the floor level of Room 5 was the same as that of the gallery, and the floors of Rooms 7 and 8 remain at that level to this day. So clearly later on (probably in the mid-fourth century for reasons presented below), the floor level of Room 5 was raised by the insertion of the hypocaust supporting the mosaic (explaining the blocking of the doorway), and at the northern end of the wing a similar thing happened with the insertion of the hypocausts and plunge pools of the West baths. The raising of the floor levels necessitated the construction of the steps into Room 5 and the north baths respectively, placed onto the existing gallery mosaic. From the mid-fourth century most of the rooms in this range were

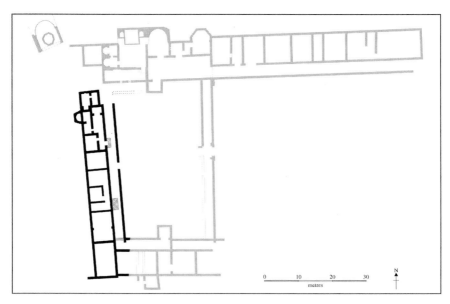

6. Plan of the west range. (*Henry Buglass/University of Birmingham*)

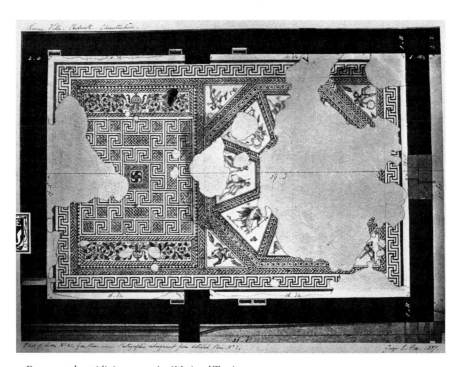

7. Room 5, the *triclinium*, mosaic. (*National Trust*)

floored with mosaic, again an indication of its importance. In addition, it is certain that the west range and the north wing had much in common and were significantly different from the south wing. These two wings contained a considerable number of rooms with mosaic floors and some with hypo-causts for heating, features that the part of the south wing opening onto the inner courtyard noticeably lacked. The lavish provision of mosaics makes it clear that the north wing and the west range were designed and decorated to impress the owner's visitors and guests; whereas the south wing, as already argued, was probably a service area, as will be seen below. So here the north and west wings will be considered together in an attempt to analyse how they were used and who used them.

In the two wings there are three sets of rooms linked by their functions. In the west range the southern end is occupied by the large Room 5 (see colour plate 2), whose plan and appointments, in particular the large, elaborate and high-quality mosaic (discussed further in Chapter 5), show that it was the dining room or *triclinium*. This had been enlarged from the 'early villa' form of the room by knocking through the south gable wall and constructing an extension, with the stubs of the earlier wall remaining as a pair of responds marking the transition from the smaller to the larger part of Room 5. This would have been a classic place in late Roman show architecture for columns framing the opening. The new, smaller part of Room 5 would have housed the dining furniture on the plainer, geometric portion of the mosaic, with the more elaborate figured mosaic of the larger part visible to the diners. Room 5a at the south end of the range housed the furnace for heating Room 5 and was probably also a fuel store.

To the north of the dining room lay what was originally, in all likelihood, a single room stretching as far as the south wall of Room 8 when it was first laid out. It was floored in mosaic of a simple, geometrical pelta plan. This mosaic only survived at its southern end where it had later been cut into to build the wall creating the new, small antechamber to the dining room (Room 5b); the mosaic had been crudely patched in white tesserae along the south face of this new wall. Excavation of the hypocaust in Room 5 showed that at one stage this continued north under Room 5b, but how far north it extended we do not know. The original large room was further subdivided, probably at the same time, by the insertion of another L-shaped wall to create the smaller room conventionally labelled Room 6, also accessed through Room 5b. When Room 6 was created it was provided with a hypocaust over which lay a polychrome mosaic floor, though only the borders survive and what the design in the centre of the floor consisted of is unknown. The insertion of Room 6 left a small lobby (Room 6a) inside the doorway from Room 5b, which was floored with a simple, rectilinear patterned mosaic. What had been the northern part of the original large room (conventionally labelled Room 7) yielded thousands of tesserae when excavated in 2000, though none was *in situ*. It is conceivable that it contained the northern end of the pelta pattern mosaic of Room 5b.

North again lies what we now see as a narrow room cut out of the north end of Room 7 by the insertion of a cross-wall, what seems to have been little more than a corridor across the west range; in excavation in 2000 some tesserae were found, but were loose and scattered. However, its southern wall does not appear on the earliest, nineteenth-century plans of the villa, raising the suspicion that it is of more recent construction and that thus the corridor did not exist in the Roman building. Room 8 remains problematic. Excavations in the 1950s and 2000s did not reveal any mosaics or substantial floors, despite the room's lying on the main axis of the villa. It seems to have been a room belonging to the 'early villa' and its earliest floor was of burnt limestone lumps. Pieces of painted wall plaster were also found in these deposits. The construction of the baths to the north led to a stokehole being pierced in the north wall. A limestone block in the north-east corner suggested to earlier excavators that this was a threshold leading to the baths, so the room has conventionally been seen as the changing room (*apodyterium*) for the baths. Nevertheless, recent excavations have shown there was no

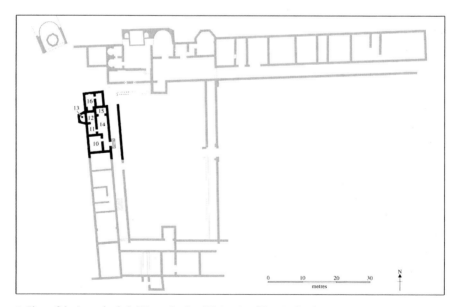

8. Plan of the 'west baths'. (*Henry Buglass/University of Birmingham*)

door before the block was put there, and Victorian restoration has obscured whether there was one after, so it is not at all clear that Room 8 was connected to the baths. At the same level as the 'threshold' were the remains of a Roman floor in mortar with much crushed tile giving a red colour to it (*opus signinum*), serviceable but not decorative.

The West Baths

At the northern end of the west range a bath suite had been inserted into the existing 'early villa' building (see colour plate 3), consisting of Rooms 10 to 15 with the furnace added to the north (Room 16). These baths are clearly a modification of the 'early villa' rooms at the time of the upgrading of the west range, as is shown by the purpose-building of the furnace at the northern end and the fact that the drain from the cold plunge bath was cut through the west gallery mosaic. The bath suite was entered by its own set of steps, suggesting it may not have connected with the rest of the range. It was floored almost throughout in polychrome mosaic. Upon entering from the gallery, there was a lobby with a simple, geometric mosaic. Immediately in front was the door into a square room (Room 10) with a hypocaust and floored with a coloured mosaic whose design consisted essentially of a St Andrew's cross or saltire, with a circular medallion containing a two-handled cup (*cantharus*) in the centre, the whole lying within a geometric border. This room has been interpreted as the changing room (*apodyterium*), which is entirely possible.

The lobby then led north to a small, rectangular room (Room 14) with a simple, geometric mosaic. This room had no hypocaust so was presumably the unheated room (*frigidarium*) with the cold plunge (Room 15) at its northern end. Opening off it to the north was Room 12, which was in fact two rooms, the long, narrow rectangle of the room being divided in two halfway along by a cross-wall (see colour plate 4). Both small rooms thus created had hypocausts with the floors supported on stacks of bricks. The mosaic in the southern room has survived, consisting of a simple (and not very well executed) geometric design within a broad, plain red border; this room will have been the warm room (*tepidarium*). The northern room, closest to the furnace, was the hot room (*caldarium*), with a small apse added on its western side to contain a plunge bath, whose warmed water would have helped maintain the steamy atmosphere of the baths. The floor of the hot room has not survived, though none of the excavators has ever mentioned the remains of mosaic collapsed into the hypocaust, so it may have been made of stone flags (later recovered for reuse). How the baths were used will be discussed in Chapter 5.

THE NORTH WING

Like the west range, the north wing originated in the 'early villa' period with a main block consisting of Rooms 26 to 29a, with detached from them to the west the original, small version of the north baths. The main block received a fronting gallery, presumably at the time of the 'great rebuilding'. Later on, Rooms 30 to 32 were added to the eastern end of the main block, fronted by an extension of the gallery. This addition cannot be dated save that it is later than the 'great rebuilding', but a date around the middle of the fourth century seems reasonable, possibly in association with the major changes we have seen to the west range. To the west of the main block, the north baths followed a complicated structural sequence we shall look at in a moment. Between them and the main block was inserted a suite of rooms consisting of Rooms 24, 24a, 25, 25a and the probable large room to the south ('in front') of them, Room 25b. The remains of the north wing will be described and discussed from west to east, starting with the north baths.

The North Baths

The western end of the north wing, adjacent to the west baths, was also a bath suite (Rooms 20 to 24) with its furnace (Room 19) added to the west end of the range (this area is one where there are very few room numbers in relation to the actual amount of rooms). The two furnace areas (Rooms 16 and 19) must have impacted on the view up to the *nymphaeum* from the inner courtyard, with Room 16 at the northern end of the west range almost closing off access, so the significance of the *nymphaeum* might have changed as the fourth century wore on. The history of the bath suite in the northern range is very difficult to disentangle, partly because earlier excavators could not dismantle the walls as they went along so they had to work in restricted areas. This meant that the walls of earlier phases were only seen in keyhole excavations and were not always understood at the time. It is also partly because the twentieth-century consolidation and restoration of the walls has given the walls new, uniform facings and thus obscured which were the earliest walls, which were subsequent additions and alterations, and the order in which these occurred.

So far as can be reconstructed, the earliest, first-phase baths consisted of two heated rooms side by side under the later Room 21a, with their stoke-holes pointing east. In the second phase the western parts of these were then incorporated into the warm room of a conventional set of damp-heat baths,

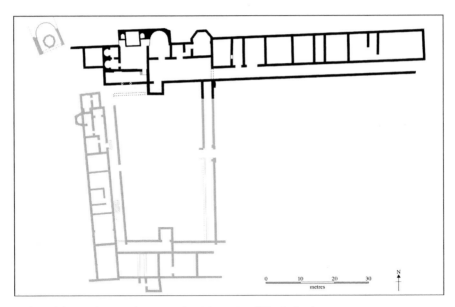

9. Plan of the north wing. (*Henry Buglass/University of Birmingham*)

with the hot room to its west fed from the new furnace at the west end of
the wing (Room 19); this furnace had strengthened sides, probably to support
a tank for heating water which would have been carried over the stokehole
itself on the three large iron bars found in excavation. The warm and hot
rooms each had a small plunge bath on its southern side. As with the baths
in the west range, it was the insertion of the hypocausts that necessitated the
raising of the floor levels and consequently the need to approach the baths up
steps. In a third phase the hot room was improved by being divided into two
small square rooms, each with a semicircular plunge bath on its western side,
the main parts of the rooms being floored with simple geometric mosaics
linked by a threshold panel in the opening between them. The main furnace
and stokehole to the west were rebuilt and reduced, and a new stokehole built
through the north wall of the new northern bath. It has been argued that
Room 24, with its apse and hypocaust, immediately to the east of the warm
room was also part of this phase of the baths, but this is by no means certain.

With the suppression of the two plunge baths on the southern side, it
may well have been now that the gallery space (Room 20) was created. This
appears to have been the exception that proved the rule about the galleries; it
does seem to have had an open, colonnaded front since three columns were
found here in the 1860s (see the columns still *in situ* albeit re-erected). It was
not floored with mosaic, however, so that constraint did not apply. It would

have formed a distinctive and architecturally ambitious frontage to the north baths; next to it was the small projecting chamber mentioned above, which might have been some sort of viewpoint.

The final fourth phase apparently saw a radical restructuring and change of the type of bath suite. What had been the warm room had its hypocaust filled in and a new floor of *opus signinum* laid; the room now served as the changing room and a circulation area. To the west the pair of former hot, damp rooms was retained, but the old, main western furnace and stokehole was abandoned, retaining the smaller northern one. The plunges of the preceding phase were knocked together, filled in and the floor level raised, leaving only a restricted space for hot air to circulate under this end of the bath suite. On the northern side of the main room new cold plunge baths were added, consisting of a central square plunge with smaller apsidal ones to either side; these were divided from the main plunge by a low wall with small columns on it, so the three spaces interconnected. The lateral, apsidal baths could only have held a single person; the larger, central one more than that. This major restructuring of the bath suite turned it from one of the common damp-heat types (what we think of as Turkish baths) to one using dry heat (more like the modern sauna). The Romans referred to this type of baths as a *laconicum* (Laconian baths), a reference to the part of Greece that was home to the Spartans, as one needed Spartan fortitude in discomfort to endure the very hot, dry conditions. For one villa to have baths of both types (rather than a hot, dry room attached to a normal damp-heat bath) was a mark of luxury, and as there is heavy wear on the stylobate (base stones) of the colonnade (Room 20) on the direct line between the doors of the two bath suites, it looks as though they were in use together.

The Reception Rooms

The complex of rooms between this set of baths to the west and the long terrace of the north wing to the east deserves more attention than it has perhaps had in the past (see colour plate 5). These rooms are the ones conventionally labelled: Room 24, a square room with a deep, slightly stilted semicircular apse (stilted: the apse has straight sidewalls before turning into the semicircle) and apparently originally with a mosaic; Room 25, a near-square room with an apse consisting of three angled walls, the whole heated by a channelled hypocaust; and between these two the smaller Rooms 24a and 25a, the former of which was heated by a hypocaust. In front of these was a large rectangular space, which was not originally given a number but which it is proposed should be called Room 25b, certainly extending across the front of

Rooms 25 and 25a, quite possibly across the front of Rooms 24a and 24, thus all the way to the east wall of the baths. In that case the projecting chamber would have been at the junction between this space and the colonnaded Room 20: there may have been a cross-wall separating Room 20 which was open to the elements from this space, which was enclosed. In support of the idea of a single, large room are fragments of a geometric mosaic that were found in the eastern half of the room, and it would be possible to extrapolate the design to fill a space of these dimensions (17m x 6m).

Their proximity to the north baths, the fact that some of them were heated and also the fact that heated, apsidal rooms were common in baths makes it understandable that Rooms 24, 24a, 25 and 25a have previously been thought of in relation to the baths. Yet there is another possibility: that they functioned separately from the baths. In this case, one could imagine Room 25b as a large, general-purpose assembly room with the two apsidal rooms, 24 and 25, as reception rooms opening off it. An apsidal form is very common for an important type of room in late Roman aristocratic residences, for example the *aula*, or formal reception room (this will be discussed in more detail in the following chapter). If this were the case, and if the northern end of the cross-gallery communicated with the large room with the geometric mosaic, visitors of insufficient status could be conducted straight to the *aula* without needing to penetrate any further into the inner courtyard.

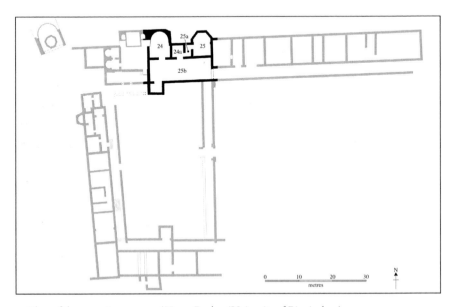

10. Plan of the reception rooms. (*Henry Buglass/University of Birmingham*)

The Residential Area

The line of the wall dividing Room 25 from Room 26 seems to have marked the division between the group of rooms just discussed and the rest of the north wing, Rooms 26 to 32. This line was prolonged by a large threshold stone across the gallery at this point and the mosaic in the north gallery is different to that in the area just discussed in front of Rooms 24, 24a, 25 and 25a; there could well have been a doorway at this point to control access to the eastern part of the north wing. Rooms 26, 26a, 27, 28, 29 and 29a are reckoned together to have formed one of the buildings of the 'early villa'. A polychrome, geometric mosaic has been uncovered at the western end of the gallery, and whether this extended all the way to the far eastern end of the gallery is unknown; if it did it must have been laid at or after the construction of the extension to the wing.

Some of the rooms in this part of the north wing had hypocausts, so their floors would have been at a higher level than that of the gallery. Unlike the west range these had been designed in from the start so it was possible to avoid simply placing a set of steps onto and partially obscuring the mosaic. Instead, a narrow passage was placed to one side of the room with the hypocaust, opening off the gallery and presumably with steps up to it to manage the change of level; Room 26a served Room 26 in this way. Room 29a seems to be of the same type, but there is no record that Room 29 ever had a hypocaust. In this case one might consider the possibility that the north wing had an upper storey and that Room 29a (and possibly Room 26a also) housed staircases to the upper floor, though it should be recognised that good evidence for upper floors in the buildings of Roman Britain is rare, so it remains no more than a possibility.

We shall work along the rooms in this part of the north wing from west to east: in Room 26 the floor was supported by a hypocaust that consisted of a forest of closely spaced, small, monolithic pillars, rather than the more usual channelled hypocaust or stacks of bricks. The stokehole ran through the western wall so the furnace would have been where Room 25 was later constructed, obliterating it. Curiously, there is little sign that the hypocaust was ever heated since the cheeks of the stokehole and the hypocaust pillars lack the characteristic reddening produced by heat; the redness being caused by the oxidisation of the iron in the limestone. What the floor supported on the hypocaust pillars consisted of we do not know. Room 27 was a room opening directly off the gallery and was not provided with a hypocaust. We know little else about it. Room 28 was larger than the rooms to either side of it and was originally floored with a polychrome mosaic of which only fragments of geometric border panels survive. These are of poor workmanship and it has been suggested that this is a late mosaic in the sequence at Chedworth, perhaps from the late fourth century. About Room 29 and its accompanying Room 29a we again know little. Rooms 30 to 32 represent an extension to the north wing, as long again as Rooms 29 to 29a. This extension would have required the most engineering in order to create the stable terrace able to carry the building and to allow for the creation of hypocausts. As we shall see, the creation of the elevated vantage point represented by the eastern end of the extended wing, Room 32, was probably designed for effect. The extension would also, of course, have made the north wing even more imposing to someone in the outer courtyard down below.

The entire extension can be interpreted as a new dining suite, with essentially the same ingredients as the Room 5 dining suite in the west range. Room 30 seems to have been the kitchen since it has an oven base in its south-west corner. Near the south-eastern corner, up against the east wall, was a pit containing food debris, including the bones of the three main food animals of the Roman period in Britain, cattle, sheep and pig, and also the bones of domestic and wild fowl. Room 31 is of uncertain function, though it might have corresponded to a room such as Room 6 in the west range suite. It seems at some stage to have had a wooden floor that burnt, since traces of it were recovered upon excavation. Room 31a looks analogous to Room 5a as the lobby or antechamber to the dining room proper and floored with a black-and-white mosaic. It did not run the full width of the

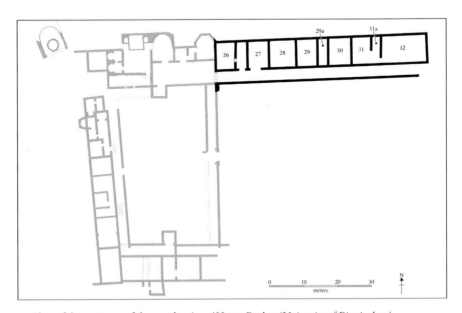

11. Plan of the east part of the north wing. (*Henry Buglass/University of Birmingham*)

range because of the use of the northern part as a furnace area for Room 32. The latter was a large, bipartite room, both parts heated by a channelled hypocaust. The larger, western part of Room 32 had its stokehole at a north-western angle, feeding in from the furnace carved from the northern end of the passage Room 31a; the eastern part had a stokehole through the east wall. The eastern part of Room 32, approximately one-third of the entire area at present is raised above the level of the western part, forming a sort of dais, but from recent re-examination it is clear that much of this part fo the room has been rebuilt in modern times, probably to counter slippage down the slope. If so, then the 'dais' may be a result of this modern activity, and indeed there is no trace of it on the earliest published plan of the villa in Grover's report of 1868. Small pieces of mosaic recovered collapsed into the hypocaust channels show that the room originally had a fine mosaic floor. Room 32 has always been interpreted as a dining room or *triclinium*, similar in layout to Room 5, except that here the area for the couches and tables was somewhat raised. This latter is now highly questionable and the identification of the room as a *triclinium* is not secure. Nevertheless, the overall plan of the suite of rooms would still allow an interpretation as a dining-suite similar to Rooms 5, 5b and 6.

Duplication of dining rooms is a feature of the wealthiest Roman residences. Often the reason would seem to be to provide a summer and a winter dining suite. This could well be the case at Chedworth, with the smaller, enclosed Room 5 as the winter suite and the larger Room 32 for summer, its ambience much enhanced by any large windows or openings giving onto what would have been an impressive view over the Coln valley and the landscape beyond. That this proposed summer dining room had a hypocaust to heat it might seem odd, but as noted before the Chedworth villa lies in a fairly cold spot, so a hypocaust could have been a prudent provision. There are other possibilities, such as a women's dining suite, which will be further considered in the next chapter. Even if we are not always sure about what went on in each of the rooms of the north wing, from Room 26 eastwards, there is one final point that should be made about this wing overall. Standing on the northern side of the valley it faced south and was thus the sunniest and warmest part of the villa, probably reinforced by its raised level. Also, if the opposite slopes were not as thickly wooded as they are now, then the sun would have been less screened. Matters of prospect, outlook and exposure to the sun are regularly referred to by aristocratic Roman writers when describing either their actual houses or the desirable qualities of a house, so Chedworth fits into this tradition very well.

THE SOUTH WING

Whereas the full extent of the north and west wings is preserved, for the south wing we only know about the part that fronts onto the inner courtyard and a small area of the lower part of the wing fronting onto the outer courtyard. The eastern part of the south wing on the upper courtyard comprises one of the buildings of the 'early villa'. The excavated part consists of a large room, Room 1, flanked by two smaller ones, Rooms 1a and 1b. The latter have floors of the reddish *opus signinum*; the floor of Room 1 is unknown. The eastern wall of Room 1a is on the same line as the eastern side of the cross-gallery and at this point there seems to be a pronounced drop to what would be the next room to the east. The steepening slope is also reflected in the south wing gallery where there is a considerable drop defined by a retaining wall across the gallery on the line of the east wall of the projection, Room 2, presumably with steps up. These three earlier rooms were linked to the west range by a single large room, Room 3. Against its western wall was a large oven base and this, combined with the fact that the doorway of Room 3 lay opposite the southern end of the west range gallery and thus had access to the Room 5 dining suite, has resulted in this room being interpreted as the kitchen for Room 5.

Behind Room 3 a smaller room, Room 4, projected south from the main line of the south wing. This was a latrine, identifiable by the characteristic Roman arrangement of a seat, here built in stone, over a sewer, running along the south wall. The seat would have had a bench along the top with a series of holes, possibly also smaller holes in the front. In front of the seat was a shallow guttering in which ran the water that overflowed from a stone basin in the north-west corner of the room and which was served by a piped supply; the gutter then discharged into the sewer at the eastern side of the room. The water in the gutter was for washing the sponges on sticks that served as toilet paper; the use of these would account for the smaller holes along the front of the seat (see colour plate 6). To us, putting a large latrine next to a kitchen seems very odd and unhygienic, but the Romans did not understand the link between waste matter and disease. If the latrine was for the use of all the inhabitants of the villa then its position is a little odd, since everyone, including the owner and his family, would have had to access it through the kitchen. The south wing joined the west range by means of Room 5a, the furnace and fuel store for Room 5, the dining room.

The Victorian excavators made no attempt to trace any continuation of the south wing east of the portion fronting onto the inner courtyard. A small

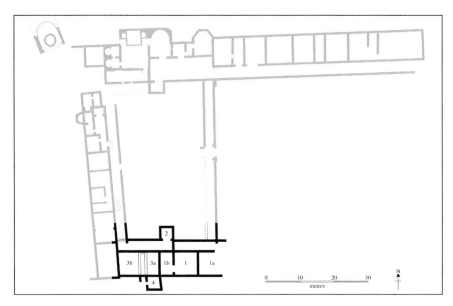

12. Plan of the south wing. (*Henry Buglass/University of Birmingham*)

13. The latrine. (*National Trust*)

14. The excavations on the lower part of the south wing. (*National Trust*)

trench excavated in 1983, south-east of the shooting lodge, showed that there were Roman walls running east–west in this area, suggesting that more of the south wing remains to be found. This trench was followed up in 1997 and an 8m stretch of the lower south wing investigated near its eastern end. The overall layout was very similar to the excavated parts of the villa, a gallery fronting a range of rooms. The gallery had no trace of a surviving floor, but it did seem to have a simple, channelled hypocaust. This is most unusual as it is very rare for galleries rather than rooms to be heated. Part of a room to the south of the gallery was excavated and this also had a channelled hypocaust, but as with the gallery, no trace of flooring survived. The presence of a hypocaust in the room and possibly in the gallery shows that this part of the south wing was destined for human occupation, and in some comfort, and was not an ancillary range such as stabling or storage as had previously been proposed. It does show that there is a large element of the accommodation in the villa still unexcavated.

THE *NYMPHAEUM* & ITS WATER

Set at the highest point of the villa complex was the *nymphaeum*, the artificial basin that captured the water of the natural spring and the building over it where the nymph of the spring could be honoured (see colour plate 7). We have already seen how the north wing and the west range did not join and how the difference in alignment between the two ranges meant that the *nymphaeum* was visible to and a focal point for anyone entering the inner courtyard through the gatehouse. The spring was identified in the previous chapter as a determining factor in the choice of site for the villa, but the religious importance of the spring and of this area for the villa is made plain by the prominence accorded to it in the overall layout and by the provision of its cover-building. Originally, the spring was channelled into a reservoir sited beneath the south-western part of the later building. This was superseded when the *nymphaeum* was built over it, with the spring now captured in a stone-lined chamber and led through the western side of the apse of the new building and thence channelled into an octagonal basin. From this a lead pipe took the water to a stone trough which was probably the distribution point. The *nymphaeum* was an elegant little building, open towards the villa, and the opening was presumably framed by columns (a column found in the basin was probably one of these) with a pediment or arch on top of them (see colour plate 8). The structure consisted of a rectangular fore part which contained the basin, with a semicircular apse as the rear part. The walls could well have been plastered and painted and there was probably a statue or a painting of the nymph in the apse. An altar with no inscription on it was found buried in the north-eastern corner. Echoes of the religious controversies of the late Roman period are shown through the chi-rho, the Christian symbol (see Chapter 4), that was found inscribed into three of the basin coping stones, so presumably the shrine was Christianised. Later still these stones were ripped up and two of them reused as building material in the north wing baths.

As well as having a sacred quality, the water from the spring was put to a series of eminently practical purposes; the fact that the spring was at the highest point of the villa meant that water could be fed throughout the complex by means of gravity. One obvious and important use was to supply the two bath suites, with the water needed for the plunge baths as well as for the water heater in the north baths, and casual use for washing and sluicing the bathers down. Part of this system can still be seen in the north baths where remains of pipes serving the small western and eastern baths of the *laconicum* version are visible. The route of the supply for the west range baths is not known, but the plunge bath emptied into a drain that was cut through the gallery mosaic and then out into the inner courtyard. How the earlier phases of the north baths drained we do not know, but for the latest, *laconicum*, phase there is some evidence.

The three baths on the north side of the bath suite all interconnected by means of pipes, so the water level in all three would remain the same. There is an outlet pipe in the north-east angle of the central plunge bath, so equally all three baths could be drained at the same time. Where this water went is uncertain. Issuing out of the north wall of the north wing, it would have needed to be led along the outside face of the wall and thence drained downhill; otherwise the water would have simply pooled up on the northern side of the wall, causing instability to the wall itself and to the slope above. The obvious and likely solution is that it was led round the western end of the north range to discharge downslope. Excavations in the inner courtyard have revealed stone-lined and-covered water channels running north to south across the courtyard. Some may have been channels directly from the trough at the *nymphaeum* bringing clean water to the south wing, perhaps for the kitchen. Others may have been the drain for the water from the north baths. This 'dirty' water could have been put to a second use flushing the sewer of the latrine behind the kitchen; the water basin and the gutter in the latrine could have been the destination for a 'clean' water duct. The effluent from the

15. Lead water-pipe. (*Graham Norrie/ University of Birmingham*)

latrine presumably discharged through the east wall and ran off downslope behind the south wing. Previously it was noted that if the latrine was for the use of the entire household then it meant everyone traipsing through the kitchen at whatever hour; yet there is no evidence for the provision of sanitary facilities anywhere else in the excavated portion of the villa, not even in the baths, which is where latrines were often sited because of the availability of running water to flush them. Of course, there could have been other provisions less visible to us, such as chamber pots, but this does evoke perhaps a different and more malodorous side to the experience of life than that of the sophisticated architecture and the colourful mosaics.

Having in this chapter laid out the physical facts of the layout of the villa overall, and the use of the various areas and rooms, so far as we can reconstruct them, it is to the experience of using the villa in the mid- to later fourth century that the next chapter will be devoted.

THREE

EXPERIENCING THE LATE ROMAN VILLA

A visitor arriving at the Chedworth villa in the later fourth century would have had a very strong impression of the physical presence of the complex, an impression utterly different from that of the modern visitor (see colour plate 9). The Roman visitor would have entered from the east, the mouth of the little valley in which the villa sat; they would thus have been at the lowest point of the valley. Above them, on either side, would have stood the great masses of the north and south ranges, the north range in particular terraced out from the hillside up to 5m (15ft) above the floor of the valley. In front of them would have risen the steep slope up to the cross-gallery that closed the western end of the outer courtyard and controlled access to the inner courtyard. At the end of the vista lay the bulk of the west wing, overtopping the cross-gallery and dominating the valley (rather as the modern cover-building does now). Above the ranges of the villa, the sides and end of the valley rose still further, creating a strong sense of enclosure and isolation from the landscape around, with the villa buildings as the focus of the visitor's field of view. It is important to recognise how very specific and purposeful the ancient experience was, since the present-day experience of the site is very different; the construction of the shooting lodge has altered the contours of the valley and the modern visitor enters not at the mouth of the valley, but up the valley's side past the latrines and through the Roman kitchens. What would have been a defining moment of any visit to the villa, arriving at it, seeing it and under-standing the impression it was intended to create, is lost for today's visitor.

That the impression was intentional and that a great deal of labour and expense had gone into creating it cannot be doubted. The area now occupied by the inner courtyard seems naturally to have been a relatively level space, and it was there, in proximity to the spring, that the core of the 'early villa' developed. Any development of the villa beyond that rather restricted area would mean tackling the problems posed by the steep slopes of the northern and southern sides of the valley, and the steep slope down to the floor of the valley at the eastern end of the level area. The owners of the fourth-century villa and their builders chose to regard the shape of the valley as an opportu-nity for a display of wealth and power rather than as a constraint. The principal buildings of the villa remained grouped around the flatter land at the head of the valley, the west wing and the neighbouring 'inner' ends of the north and south ranges. The creation of the cross-gallery linking the north and south ranges and closing off the eastern side of the head of the valley emphasised the separation of the inner part of the villa partly by its physical presence as a screen, but also because it was terraced into the slope, creating a vertical face to the outer courtyard. At the same time, it performed an important structural function by revetting the slope and thereby shoring up the area of the inner courtyard. The part of the south wing fronting onto the inner courtyard was naturally at the same upper level as the other buildings around the courtyard, but what we know of the range east of the cross-gallery shows that it was constructed at a lower level, using the natural slope of the valley side (we do not know whether the lower and upper parts of the range communicated directly or were blocked off from each other).

For the north wing, the 'early villa' building had been terraced into the hillside. When the galleries were constructed to unify the ranges architectur-ally, the one for the north wing was set immediately in front of the existing building on a terrace. Later the decision was taken to extend the north wing further to the east. In order to do this, it was necessary to construct an arti-ficial terrace along the northern side of the valley to carry the extension to the range at the same level as the part giving onto the inner courtyard. To do this the terrace was created partly by cutting back into the hillside and partly by building up a level platform jutting out over the lower part of the valley. Like the cross-gallery, this would have had a steep or even vertical face rising up from the outer courtyard. The Roman visitor would instantly have grasped the major difference between the buildings, such as the eastern part of the south range, that were at the lower level and easily accessible from the outer courtyard, compared with those that towered above and could only be entered through the gatehouse in the centre of the cross-gallery. To access the inner courtyard would have meant moving up to the gatehouse in the cross-gallery; unfortunately, the construction of the nineteenth-century shooting lodge has obliterated this part of the villa so we do not know whether there was just a slope, a ramp or a monumental stairway up to the gatehouse. From the gatehouse to the inner court was another short flight of steps.

Once the visitor had mounted to the inner courtyard there was still a series of different levels to be negotiated, partly the result of the natural slope and of practical considerations, but probably partly to do with emphasising or downplaying different parts of the ranges around the courtyard. Due to the natural slope down from west to east the west range was always going to be the furthest upslope, and anyone approaching it from the gate in the cross-gallery would have had to walk a short way up the slope. As it was originally constructed early in the fourth century and the floor level of the west range was probably all at the level of the gallery along the facade of the range; that is, the level of the surviving gallery mosaic (see colour platr 10). However, with the major reconstruction of the west range around the middle of the fourth century, the insertion of hypocausts to create the new bath suite at the northern end of the wing and a hypocaust under the new mosaic in the dining room, much of the range was necessarily raised 1m (3ft) or so above the previous level. This now meant that there had to be steps up into these rooms, and these were made of limestone blocks placed onto the existing mosaic with no regard for its patterning.

The highest part of the range was the dining room (Room 5) towards the southern end and there were five steps from the southern end of the gallery into the dining area. Rooms 6, 7 and 8 in the centre of the range stepped down from the level of the dining room and the bath suite was not raised as high as the southern end, so there are only two steps up into it. Overall, the north wing seems to have lain a little lower than the west range, responding to the natural west–east slope. It seems likely that as originally constructed, adapting the existing 'early villa' building, the floor levels were all at the same height. It was the insertion of the hypocausts to heat the north baths, along with the subsequent remodelling of these baths, that caused them to rise relative to the rest of the wing (these are discussed in Chapter 2) and thus to make this part of the site rather confusing for the modern visitor.

The south wing, by contrast, lies lower than the north and west ones. In part this is a consequence of the natural slope, but since, as we shall see below, the south wing appears to be a much more workaday 'service' wing, its lower physical position could be seen to reflect its lower functional and social status. This was marked at the angle between the south wing and the west range by the short flight of steps up from the plain southern gallery to the western gallery with its mosaics; the transition being further marked by the doorway near the southern end of the western gallery, where the mosaic ended. Halfway along the surviving stretch of the southern gallery was another flight of steps and there were changes in level within Room 1, though these may have been to do with managing the increasingly steep slope in this area. Of course, the highest point in the whole ensemble was taken by the *nymphaeum* and the spring, emphasising the importance of the sacred elements of the landscape, natural and man-made.

Chedworth's builders deliberately managed and profited from the natural form of the site to create a very distinctive experience for the members of the household and for visitors. This exploitation of changes in levels to create an experience, even if sometimes subliminal rather than conscious, is one that can be detected at other late Roman villas, though seldom as markedly as at Chedworth, making this aspect one of the most distinctive and unusual features of the villa. Perhaps the closest parallel to Chedworth lies in the villa at Great Witcombe, only some 15km (10 miles) to the west (see colour plate 11). Lying at the foot of the Cotswold scarp, Great Witcombe also had and profited from a very sloping site. The overall layout of the excavated part of this villa was in the form of a U, with the cross-range at the highest part of the slope and consisting of little more than a buttressed gallery with the main reception room behind it on the axis of the complex. The two side wings ran downslope with sets of steps in the galleries managing access between the different levels. Again, the natural topography of the site was being used to impress, with the main range highest up so that the most important room and personages were set above all others and access to them involved physical effort as well as social constraints. Even more impressive was a villa the other side of the country at Castor, just to the west of modern Peterborough. Here, a massive villa ran down a steep slope in a series of terraces, sometimes with substantial retaining walls, the summit of the hill being crowned by the substantial buildings of the principal range which would have commanded extensive views out over the surrounding landscape to the south and also to the east and west; equally, it would have been very visible from round about, probably being the dominant feature in most views. Yet the large-scale management of levels to create an effect was in fact a rarity in Britain, making Chedworth one of a small group of residences of this class. By contrast, the grandest of all the late Roman villas in the Cotswolds, the one at Woodchester near Stroud, some 25km (15 miles) south-west of Chedworth, eschewed the potential of the steep hill-slopes there in favour of the flat valley bottom, where the huge complex could be laid out much more symmetrically and with a pronounced axis leading from the outside world to the grand reception rooms.

Axiality was the other dominating feature of the layout of Chedworth, one of which we are perhaps more conscious since our plans of the villa are two-dimensional, masking the significance of the contours of the site. The symmetry is not perfect, however, particularly as regards the west range, so there is a tension between axiality and other factors. The north and south wings are long and parallel, creating a strong east–west axis; with the eastern end of the complex open and the western end closed off by the west range, the spatial logic of the complex is strongly axial with the axis leading to the centre of the west range. Nevertheless, as seen in Chapter 2, the west range is not at right angles to the north and south wings, but lying almost due north–south, its north end inclined somewhat to the west of where it should be; this also means the west range and the north wing did not physically join at the angle. This nonconformity of the west range to a strictly axial plan has significance and raises questions. The alignment of the west range is that of the western building of the 'early villa', which continued in use; when that building was remodelled to form the west range of the fourth-century complex, the opportunity could have been taken to realign it to conform to the overall axis, but it was not. This could have been partly for reasons of economy, but economy is not noticeably the guiding principle of the fourth-century patrons. This suggests that keeping the alignment mattered.

What the arrangement does is use the north end of the west range and the west end of the north wing to frame the *nymphaeum* on its little knoll, so it looks as though the religious importance of the spring and its guardian deities was sufficient to cause a 'deformation' of any formal layout of the villa (see colour plate 12). This framing effect is particularly evident when entering the inner courtyard from the gatehouse in the cross-gallery, but the gatehouse itself raises a question; it is not central in the cross-gallery and thus not directly facing the entranceway in the centre of the facade of the west range. This is unlikely to have been by accident, but why it is we cannot tell because of the shooting lodge which covers most of this part of the site. In fact, the misalignment of the gatehouse and the west range entry is slight and one may wonder whether it would have been that noticeable to the casual observer.

More important is a question raised by the logic of the overall axial arrangement of the site and from practice at other villas. Logically, there should be a major focus in the centre of the west range, the culminating point in two dimensions of the long axis of the villa and in three dimensions of the ascent from the valley bottom. This is where, in a great many Roman villas and other residences, one finds the main reception room, not only in Britain but more widely across the empire. Great Witcombe is a good local example, where behind the central gallery and on the axis of the complex there is a simple rectangular room with an apse (a common form), later replaced by an octagonal room that must have been a very impressive architectural space. At Chedworth there is no record of any imposing, lavishly decorated room in this important position. Indeed, the room immediately inside the main entranceway to the range (Room 8) is among the most unimpressive in the villa. The entrance to the range actually lines up, more or less, with the cross-wall dividing Rooms 7 and 8. One possibility would be that as at Great Witcombe the reception room lay behind (on the west side of) the west range, but none of the excavators of the villa has ever alluded to such a room. Unfortunately, the modern restoration of the back wall of the range has masked any traces of possible walls running west and forming part of such a room. Even if there were such a room, Room 8 with its lack of embellishment would be a strange antechamber to the most important room in the villa. At present the balance of probabilities would seem to argue against such a room having existed. This, of course, leaves the question of where the principal reception room was, and in Chapter 2 it was suggested that either Room 24 or Room 25 in the north wing, just to the east of the baths and fronted by the large room with a mosaic, would make a suitable candidate.

Before looking in more detail at how some of the rooms or suites of rooms were possibly used, it is worth pausing to think about the general principles that might have dictated what rooms the villa had and how they were arranged. A number of factors have been proposed as being behind the layout of a high-status Roman or Romano-British house: status, gender, age, family groupings, permutations of these and other factors such as seasonality. Currently, it is the first of these that is seen as the most important conditioning factor for Roman houses. Status should be understood in two ways: first of all, there is status within the household or the community internal to the villa; second, there is the status of visitors or guests external to the villa and how this affected their access. We have little direct evidence for the make-up of an aristocratic Romano-British household of the fourth century; we are dependent on the picture available from better-documented areas of the empire. The written sources from these areas give a consistent overall picture: of a nuclear family controlled by an adult male who was landowner (in late Roman terminology *dominus*, or lord) and head of the family. He would have had a wider household of servants and other social inferiors, as well as the labourers on his lands with their families. Again, we lack direct evidence for the legal status of these people: were they slaves or were they free, and if free, how dependent were they on the villa's proprietor? These matters are discussed in more detail in the next chapter.

From outside the villa would come visitors and guests. Differences in status in late Roman society were very precisely calibrated, and who or what you were dictated how you would be received and treated by the *dominus*, his family and household. The traditional basis of Roman status was land. As in so many societies before and since this was the measure of a lord's and a family's worth (social as well as financial), particularly if it was inherited; the Roman aristocracy had much the same attitude to 'old money' and parvenus, and indeed 'trade', as did the Victorian. The *dominus* of a villa such as Chedworth would therefore expect to receive his fellow landowners on a regular basis and to treat them according to their status. Some of these might be his social equals; others might be lower down the pecking order. At the top of the social structure remained the families that constituted the senate, the ancient order of nobility that had for so long run the Roman world, and even when shorn of its real power by the advent of emperors still enormously important in terms of wealth and influence. The great senatorial families had huge portfolios of estates scattered across the empire; in fact, the only fourth-century landowner in Britain whose name we know was just such a personage: the senatorial lady Melania the Younger (this rich woman was to pass through the eye of the needle and enter the Kingdom of Heaven as a saint). Any member of the senatorial order, or his lady or children, would be especially lavishly received.

The late Roman world, however, had other hierarchies of power and wealth that had to be accommodated alongside the traditional aristocracies of wealth; these were the hierarchies of the imperial service, the administrative, financial and military command structures. Lying not far from Cirencester, which may well have been the capital of the late Roman province of *Britannia Prima* (essentially today's West Country and South Wales), Chedworth might well have seen the provincial governor, responsible for the administration of the province and the maintenance of law and order. As representative of the emperor himself through the Vicarius of the Britains in London and thence to the Praetorian Prefect of the Gauls at the imperial seat at Trier on the Moselle, the governor was a man of power and consequence, but also a potential patron who could smooth the way to imperial favour and appointments. High officials of the financial and military commands would probably not be seen in this area that often, but tax officials and soldiers might well be, ensuring the collection of money taxes and the collection and transportation of taxes in kind, such as grain and livestock, to supply the frontier armies in the north and on the south-eastern coasts. One of the surviving finds from earlier excavations at Chedworth is a bronze buckle from a belt of the type worn either by soldiers or officials in the imperial service.

All these differences in legal and social status would have dictated to what parts of the villa an individual had access, how often, and how they would have been received and treated by the *dominus*. The immediate members of the *familia* by blood and marriage would probably have had free run of the villa, more particularly of the residential parts, though this may well have been constrained by considerations of gender and age as will be discussed below. Domestic servants or slaves would have had access to those parts of the villa in which they worked but not others, and of course their relations with the *dominus* and his family would have been utterly different to those between the *dominus* and his family. Estate labourers, tenant farmers and others would probably have been largely confined to the outer courtyard and not needed or permitted to enter the inner courtyard and the ranges of rooms around it; if they did it would have been but rarely. On the other hand, honoured guests, such as the social equals of the *dominus* or his social supe-riors such as members of the high aristocracy or the provincial governor, would have access to the formal reception rooms of the inner courtyard and there be received and entertained by the *dominus* with all due formality, as we shall see in Chapter 5. Therefore, social status was perhaps the most impor-tant key to an individual's experience of the villa. If so, then we shall need to look at who had access to different parts of the complex and how the villa was structured along the 'public–private' axis which was so important in Roman aristocratic residence.

There were also considerations such as gender and age. Many traditional societies – and in general Roman society was traditional and conservative – have to a greater or lesser degree prevented women from coming into con-tact with males not of the family or household. Our impression of Roman women, or at least of women of the higher aristocracy, is that they enjoyed a degree of autonomy and were able to interact with men from outside the *familia*; but this is a picture biased towards the aristocracy where different norms may have prevailed. On the other hand, and as we shall see in more detail in the next chapter, many women of the aristocracies at provincial level and upwards in the late Roman period were presented in public as well-dressed mirrors to their husband's wealth and status, so may well have been passive rather than active participants in some social settings. As so often, we simply do not know what the situation was in late Roman Britain, but it does pose to us the question of whether there are any parts of the Chedworth villa that might plausibly be seen as 'women's quarters' where the womenfolk of the household spent their time. Rather than seeing this type of area as a means of controlling women, one might also see it as a place where the women of the household might receive female guests, especially the womenfolk of honoured male guests, and where a parallel social world might be enacted.

There is little evidence from Roman Britain or from the Roman world generally that children had much in the way of space specifically set aside for them, in the manner of more modern nurseries. Younger children of the *dominus* and his immediate family may have stayed with their mothers, while older ones would have begun education in the ways described in the next chapter, which have left little trace in the archaeology of the villa. There is also the question of whether we can identify 'servile' or 'below-stairs' areas of the villa. As has been said, the lack of mosaics or other signs of opulence and the presence of the kitchens for the Room 5 dining suite have led to the conclusion that this was a service wing; this is in contrast to the other two wings fronting onto the inner courtyard with their plentiful mosaics and specialised areas such as the bathhouses and dining suites. Of course, in antiquity as well as the visual indicators of the status and function of a room, from such things as mosaics and wall paintings (see below), there would also have been the furniture, which as in a modern house would have declared the use of the room. No furniture survives from Chedworth, however, apart from some pieces of stone tabletops. Moreover, in Roman houses rooms did not necessarily have the fixed functions rooms in modern houses have (kitchens and latrines being an exception); neither did they necessarily 'belong' to a particular member of the household: the idea of 'so-and-so's bedroom' would probably have made little sense to an inhabitant of the Chedworth villa. Instead, rooms could change function according to how they were furnished and what time of day it was: a room that in the morning was the *aula* where the *dominus* received his guests or tenants might in the late afternoon, with a change of furniture, have acted as the dining room. Equally, people might pass the night in rooms that in the daytime had performed other functions. So to what extent may the remains of the buildings and rooms with their decoration and fixtures allow us to propose how the villa was used and how the household and guests experienced it?

Given that what survives to us is the plan of the north and west wings, the rooms in them and the presence of features such as hypocausts and mosaics, along with readily identifiable groups of rooms such as baths and dining suites, the most productive line of analysis is that of access and the public–private access.

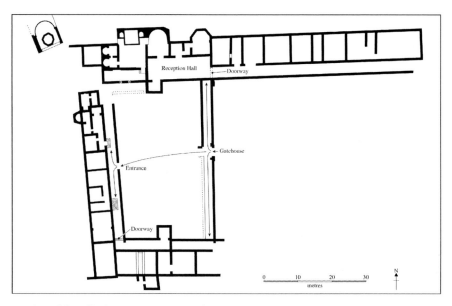

16. Plan of the villa showing access control. (*Henry Buglass/University of Birmingham*)

For this we may use the layout of the wings, the plans and fittings of the rooms within them and the invaluable evidence of which rooms were and were not floored with mosaic: mosaic, being a luxury installation, is likely to mark out those rooms which were either accessible to a large number of people or were designed to impress a more restricted and more honoured group. The broad division between the outer courtyard and the inner has been evoked several times, and there can be little doubt that many people of low status would rarely if ever have penetrated into the higher-status areas of the villa uphill.

Those who ascended to the gatehouse of the cross-gallery and were granted entrance could turn left, turn right or go straight on. If the ends of the cross-gallery did communicate with the galleries of the south and north wings, those turning left could have accessed the service areas of the south wing directly. Those turning right could have reached the large Room 25b in front of the two apsidal chambers, Rooms 24 and 25. As already noted, the apsidal form is the commonest for the *aula*, the formal reception room where the *dominus* received guests and clients, its form echoing the huge *aulae* of imperial residences, for instance at Trier, where the *dominus* of the Roman world held audience. Among those who would have been received by the *dominus* of Chedworth were his tenants and estate workers; it is likely that they were channelled to the *aula* by the shortest route possible since their status did not allow them access to other parts of the villa. The proprietor would also have needed to receive and discuss matters with the upper members of his household staff, such as his bailiff or estate(s) manager(s), responsible for the good running of his lands, or the steward, responsible for the smooth organisation of his household. We do not know whether there was in late Roman Britain anything corresponding to the system of *clientela* that had been practised at Rome, where first thing in the morning a great man's clients waited upon their patron and were given gifts in return for doing such things as voting for his preferred candidates in election, or following him when he left his house to impress by their number. If such things did occur in late Roman Britain it would perhaps have been more likely in a town such as Cirencester rather than out in the countryside.

The large, mosaic-floored Room 25b would have been an ideal space in which those seeking access to the *dominus* or who were to be greeted by him could assemble and be marshalled before being admitted to his presence. It is noticeable that both Room 24 and Room 25 were heated, and indeed stood next to the north baths, so would have been warm even in midwinter. It is possible that higher-status guests would have gone straight ahead at the gatehouse to enter the reception areas and *aula* by a different route, or it might have been the *dominus* who came to greet them; such nuances mattered. Or it might be that they were there to be entertained and thus were conducted straight to the baths or to the west range dining suite according to the time of day. The highly ritualised social behaviours that went on in these spaces will be described in Chapter 5.

Having dealt with the possible reception area in the north wing, the dining suite in the west range and the north and west baths, this leaves little in the residential areas of the villa save the part of the north wing running east from the cross-gallery and overlooking the outer courtyard. This part of the wing does seem to have been divided off from the rest of the inner courtyard areas, suggesting that it performed more private (or at least less public) functions and was therefore an area into which access was even more controlled. What went on in many of the rooms we do not know. One possibility is that these wings contained the private living quarters of the family of the *dominus*; in Chapter 2 the possibility was raised of an upper floor with Rooms 26a and 29a hosting the staircases, which would considerably enlarge the amount of accommodation. Another possibility, given the control of access to this part of the villa, is that this was where the women and children of the main family resided. It should be remembered that the eastwards extension to this wing (Rooms 30–32) seems to be a duplicate of the dining suite in the west range. The mid-fifth-century writer Sidonius Apollinaris, when describing his villa at Avitacum, somewhere near Clermont-Ferrand in central Gaul, refers in passing to a *triclinium matronale* – a women's dining room. If the eastern part of the north wing were in any sense the women's quarters of the villa, then the duplication of dining suites would make sense and be an index of the wealth of the *dominus* that his womenfolk had such a large and lavishly equipped dining suite. Another possibility, suggested in Chapter 2 and also attested in the ancient sources, is that this was a summer dining suite. Its position on the artificial terrace with views out to the landscape beyond would accord very well with what we know of the desired qualities of a summer dining room, again a tribute to the wealth and lavish entertaining rooms of the *dominus* of the Chedworth villa.

So by taking the idea of the public–private axis and the degrees of penetration allowed to different classes and types of visitor or guest, and combining with this other ideas such as the structuring of the spaces by gender, age and time of day, and possibly also by season, we can arrive at some suggestions as to why the wings and rooms of the Chedworth villa were laid out, floored and equipped in the ways they were. This is not to say that this is how it was; it may or it may not have been. But it is an exercise in showing how we might seek to understand and interpret the bare remains left to us. Of those remains, the most spectacular are the mosaics, which have been mentioned several times in both this chapter and the preceding one. It is time to consider them in more detail, and along with them the other elements of the appointments and decoration of the villa that have come down to us.

THE MOSAICS & DECORATION

The mosaics of the Chedworth villa constitute one of the largest collections of mosaics at a single Romano-British site and one of the largest now available for the visitor to inspect. Hundreds of mosaics have been found at Romano-British sites and over the past half-century have been the subject of intense study so that we are now able to discuss not just individual mosaics, but groups of mosaics related to each other by stylistic criteria and by date. The Chedworth mosaics can, therefore, be discussed both in terms of their place in the villa and by their relationship to other mosaics elsewhere. Of the eighteen mosaics identified at Chedworth, one consists of a number of loose tesserae (the cubes of coloured stone) from the lower south wing. Room 7 in the west range, when excavated in 1864, had the remains of a coloured mosaic, but by the time of re-excavation in 2000 this had disintegrated into loose tesserae. The condition of the others ranges from the fragmentary (Rooms 24, 25b, 28 and 32) to the partially preserved (Rooms 5b, 6, the lobby to the north baths, 22 and 31a) to the near-complete (Rooms 5, the lobby to Room 6, 10, 11 and 14). In addition, there are the gallery mosaics of the west and north wings: the former is now known to extend almost the whole length of the range; the latter is known only in its western part – how far east it extended is at present unknown.

The technique of creating a mosaic was in essence simple: a thick bed of mortar was prepared, with a fine coating or skim on its upper surface, and while this was still damp pieces of coloured stone were pressed into it to create the desired pattern. In the case of Chedworth, as with most Romano-British mosaics, the stone was sourced from not that far afield: stones occurring in the Cotswolds (oolites) were used for the whites, off-whites to beiges and olive greens; Lias from the area of Somerset for the blues and greys; Pennant or Old Red sandstones from south-east Wales and the Forest of Dean respectively for the purples and purple-browns. Red was usually obtained by breaking up bricks or roof tiles, and occasionally sherds of samian (a glossy red pottery) were used for detailed work, though not at Chedworth. The highest quality of mosaic was made with small (sometimes tiny) glass tesserae; none has been found at Chedworth villa, though there are records of such tesserae from one of the two possible temple sites (see Chapter 6) in the vicinity of the villa.

The range of colours used, the size of the tesserae and the quality of the workmanship in fitting them together, plus the quality of the artistry in deploying the colours to represent such things as flesh tones, are all indicators of the quality and costliness of the mosaic. For instance, at Chedworth the great dining room mosaic in Room 5 is very skilfully executed, while the remaining fragments from Room 28 suggest something far less competent. There remains considerable debate over whether mosaics, especially the more complex panels, were laid directly on site or whether they were prefabricated elsewhere and transported, being inserted into the supporting mortar or transferred off some sort of backing. That mosaics could be created on site is apparent from the fact that it is not uncommon to find mistakes, particularly in repetitive patterns where the pattern goes wrong or where it does not fit the room properly; the geometric mosaic in Room 11 in the west baths has quite a number of small mistakes, suggesting a less-than-expert mosaicist. On the other hand, when the mosaic in Room 10 was re-laid in 1978 it was observed that the mortar under its central roundel was of a different colour to that under the rest of the mosaic, so it may have been a prefabricated panel.

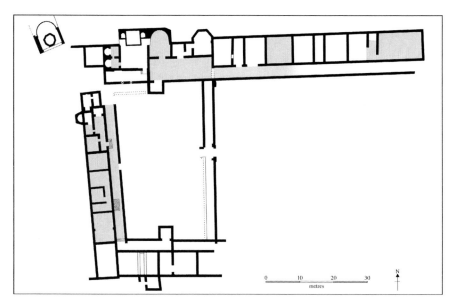

17. Plan of the villa with its distribution of mosaics. (*Henry Buglass/University of Birmingham*)

Mosaics were often suspended over hypocausts; this is the case with Rooms 5, 5b, 6, 10, 11, 14, 24, 28 and 32 at Chedworth, half of the total. Such floors were particularly prone to subsidence or even collapse during their lifetime as the weight of the mortar bedding for the mosaic (*suspensura*) and of the mosaic itself were considerable, and if it were supported on a pillared hypocaust the pillars (*pilae*) could give under the weight. This was all the more likely if hot air circulated in the hypocaust and caused the pillars to weaken; this possibly affected the mortar bedding also, particularly if the hypocausts were repeatedly heated and cooled, expanding and contracting the materials and the mortar of the hypocaust and mosaic bedding. The two best-preserved mosaics at Chedworth, in Rooms 5 and 10, show clear signs of patching, probably because of movement and subsidence. The Room 5 mosaic and others, such as those in Rooms 6, 28 and 32, have partially or wholly collapsed into the underlying hypocaust since the abandonment of the villa, when rubble and earth lying on top of them would have increased the pressure.

The majority of the Chedworth mosaics had geometric designs. This was the case for the mosaics that floored the long north and west galleries (see colour plate 13), the floor of the large Room 25b and the apsidal Room 24 opening off it, and the mosaics in the north and west baths (though that in Room 10 of the west baths is considered further below) and the fragment remaining in Room 5b. Only fragments of the large mosaics in the Room 32 dining room survive, so it is impossible to know whether, as is highly likely, there was a more complex design as in its Room 5 counterpart. The lobby to this room, Room 31a, had a geometric mosaic. The mosaic in Room 28 is too fragmentary, only parts of a geometric border surviving, so we cannot be certain what its central area contained. Room 6 in the west range had a mosaic of which the greater part has collapsed into the underlying hypocaust, leaving only a border of geometrical elements, though there could have been a figured central panel (see colour plate 14). The lobby to this room, Room 6a, had a very simple mosaic of rectangles in contrasting colours.

The mosaic of Room 10, also in the west range, is sufficiently complete for more to be said about it (see colour plate 15). This room was probably the changing room of the baths and consisted of a rectangular main panel with a saltire (St Andrew's cross) and was surrounded by geometric borders. At the centre of the saltire was a circular panel containing a *cantharus*, a two-handled cup, and in the arms of the saltire was a series of geometric motifs. The arms of the saltire and the central roundel were defined by a two-strand guilloche (braid) which joined into the lines of another two-strand guilloche defining the main panel itself. Round this was a wide border composed of swastika-meander interspersed with rectangular panels of guilloche. There was then a plain border to the room, though on the southern side there was an extra

18. The smaller part of the Room 5 mosaic. (*Luigi Thompson*)

long, thin panel of two-strand guilloche. The border was not entirely plain. To east and west it was of a darker colour stone, while to the north the outer part of the border mixed some tesserae of this darker colour in with the lighter to create a dappled effect, perhaps more interesting than just a flat panel all of the same colour. This mosaic shows signs of more than one episode of patching and restoring. Almost the entire southern half of the mosaic had to be replaced, probably because of the need to restore the hypocaust. On the whole, these repairs were less accomplished than the original work. This is particularly evident in the central medallion: above the *cantharus* is an area of white tesserae that originally formed the background, while the restoration used the more common creamy ones. Even more flagrant is the replacement of part of the southern swastika-meander panel, which is clearly a bad job. Whether this was due to declining skills on the part of the mosaicists or the owners paying for a low-grade repair, or a combination of both, we do not know. The Room 6 mosaic has lost its central part through collapse into the underlying hypocaust.

This leaves us with the splendid mosaic flooring in both parts of the west range dining room, Room 5. This comprised two unequally sized areas: a larger panel in the main part of the room, which was a room of the 'early villa', and a smaller panel in the extension knocked through the south wall of the original room; both floored with a mosaic of high artistic quality, showing a high level of technical accomplishment in the laying out and execution of the mosaic and demonstrating careful choice and use of the shape and colours of tesserae to achieve the desired effect. The smaller panel (see colour plate 16) consisted of a geometric scheme with a large, square central area where swastika-meander encloses square and rectangular panels of guilloche mat, and at the centre a square containing a 'swastika pelta'. This was flanked to east and west by rectangular strips which managed the transition from the square of the central area to the rectangle of the room; these strips contained in their centres fluted bowls from which issued scrolls of vegetation. This part of the Room 5 mosaic was enclosed by borders of two-strand guilloche and swastika-meander that also enclosed the larger part of the room, thus uniting the whole. Compared with the rich figured design of the larger panel in Room 5, the geometric decoration of the smaller panel is much more restrained. It has long been thought that this was because the diners ate here, meaning much of the mosaic would have been covered by the couch and tables. By contrast, the larger part of the room had an elaborate and sophisticated design, though sadly much of it has subsequently collapsed into the underlying hypocaust.

The larger panel (see colour plate 17) was square and inscribed into it was
an octagon, with a smaller octagon at its centre which is now lost to us. This is
a pity, since it would have contained the main figure of the composition; given
that the panels in the outer octagon have a Bacchic theme, it is almost certain
that the central octagon would have held a representation of Bacchus, the god
of wine and its effects – a god portrayed on a number of other fourth-century
mosaics from Britain. Three of the panels of the outer octagon are lost; two
show only one leg or both legs respectively of human or divine figures; the
other three survive reasonably complete. The central one of the three was the
one that would have immediately faced the diners, so it would have been the
most prominent from their viewpoint. It shows two seated figures, one male
and one female, with their bodies turned away from each other but their
heads turned back to look at one another. The implements the male figure is
holding identify him as the god Bacchus. It is thought that the female figure
is Ariadne, daughter of King Minos of Crete, who had helped Theseus kill the
Minotaur but was afterwards abandoned by him on the island of Naxos where
she was discovered by and married to Bacchus. The two panels flanking the
central one contain a satyr and a maenad, the male and female followers of
the god Dionysus, also a god of wine who by the fourth century was regularly conflated with Bacchus. Also in these panels are various objects such as
the pan pipes, tambourines and the curved staff called a *thyrsus* that were the
regular equipment of the ecstatic followers of Bacchus/Dionysus.

The four triangles between the octagon and the surrounding square are
occupied by four cupids representing the Four Seasons. Working clockwise
from the south-western corner, the first one, on the left from the viewpoint
of the diners, is Spring, naked except for a piece of gauze across his midriff
and holding a basket and the swallow of spring. In the north-western corner
is Summer, naked and holding a basket and a garland of flowers; he is the only
one shown with wings. In the north-eastern corner comes Autumn, the most
damaged of the three, like Spring naked except for a strip of material and
holding a basket; unfortunately whatever he had in his other hand has been
lost. In the south-eastern corner is Winter (see colour plate 18), probably the
most famous part of all the Chedworth mosaics. He is intact, shown muffled
up against the cold with a cloak and a hood. In his left hand he holds a leafless
branch and in his right a hare. Clearly the main panel of this mosaic, with the
octagons and the figures in them, was designed to be seen by the diners reclining in the smaller part of the room, and its figures would have been a subject
for conversation and perhaps a show of learned comment of the type described
in Chapter 5. There is a surprisingly crude repair to the border between the

figure of Summer and the octagon, where part of the two-strand guilloche has been replaced with a series of chevrons impinging onto the neighbouring bands of the mosaic.

At what date were these mosaics laid? To answer this question is not an exact science. The materials of the mosaic itself do not provide any clue, though as we shall see the designs and the motifs may. The best method is to look beneath the mosaic, for when a mosaic is lifted there may be dating evidence underneath it sealed in at the time it was laid. This does occasionally happen, especially if the area for the mosaic was prepared by dumping material to level up the area in order to receive the mortar base. In such cases there is usually some pottery, which can often be dated to within a half-century or so. More rarely there may be a coin. Coins can normally be dated at least to the reign of the emperor for whom they were issued, sometimes more precisely if, for instance, the coin tells us how many times the emperor had been consul (common on first- and second-century coins) or what anniversary of his accession it was (on fourth-century coins). However, this is the date at which the coin was struck, not when it was lost in the layers under the mosaic; it might have been in circulation for a short time or it might have been around for decades. Therefore, it can only give a date after which the layer in which it was found was formed, since it could not have been formed before the coin existed to be incorporated into it (what archaeologists learnedly call a *terminus post quem*, a date after which). But how long after? The Chedworth mosaics have been singularly unforthcoming with dating material. We can say that the mosaic in Room 5b must have been laid earlier than that in Room 6, since the construction of Room 6 cut through and truncated the Room 5b mosaic, but that is about as far as we can get on the evidence from Chedworth alone. We need to turn to other similar and better-dated mosaics to get an approximation of the date(s) of the Chedworth mosaics.

The prolonged study of the mosaics of Roman Britain has allowed scholars to define a number of regional groupings where mosaics of the same period and in the same region display a number of pronounced similarities. Quite what this corresponds to in terms of the organisation of the mosaic industry and of individual mosaicists remains unresolved. It used to be the view that these groupings represented a school (or in Latin an *officina*) of mosaicists working together and based in a particular place; indeed, it was thought that one of these schools was centred in Cirencester. Currently, the picture is of something more fluid with regional traditions, with these also combining and recombining on different projects, probably as individual mosaicists moved around from commission to commission. Nevertheless, there are two regional traditions whose main distribution centres in the Cotswolds and are both represented at Chedworth.

How are these regional traditions identified and distinguished from the products in other regions? Essentially there are three levels at which this works: first, chosen themes or personages much used in a region; second, preferred layouts or designs for mosaics; third, favoured decorative elements and motifs.

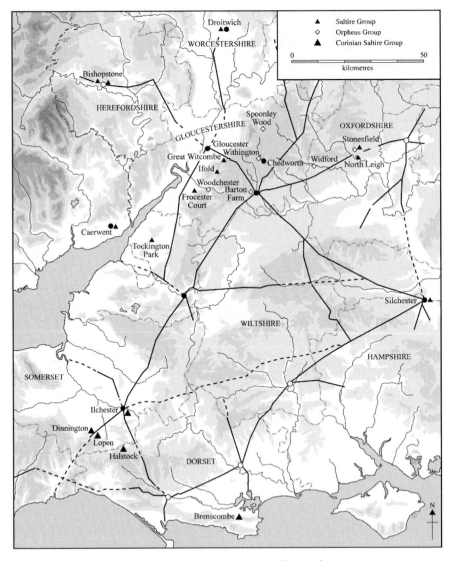

19. A map of *Corinium* mosaics. (*Henry Buglass / University of Birmingham*)

We may take these in turn in relation to the regional groupings in the Cotswolds and their appearance on particular mosaics at Chedworth. The most popular divinity to be depicted on fourth-century mosaics in Britain was Orpheus, quite possibly because of his conquest of death. The largest and most elaborate of these mosaics is the so-called Great Pavement in the Woodchester villa near Stroud (mentioned previously). This shows Orpheus surrounded by two circular registers showing animals and birds. A smaller version of this was found at the villa at Barton Farm just outside the walls of Cirencester, so not far from Chedworth. Both of these have wide borders consisting of very distinctive geometric patterns with some very particular motifs. As a result, these and other similar mosaics have recently been termed the Orpheus Group.

The work of this group appears at Chedworth in the most elaborate of all the mosaics, that in Room 5. The acanthus scroll panels in the smaller part of Room 5 are dead ringers for the acanthus scroll register that surrounds the representations of the beasts and the birds at Woodchester, and the entire central panel is a larger version of the corner panels at Woodchester; the outer swastika-meander border of this smaller part of Room 5 also has a close parallel at Woodchester. The Room 6 mosaic, though fragmentary, has enough of its border remaining to show that it uses the layout and some motifs characteristic of the Orpheus Group; it is a pity that the central part of the mosaic no longer survives. The mosaics in Room 22 in the north baths and the large Room 25b in the north wing, though also fragmentary, share the repertoire of geometric patterns and individual elements of the Orpheus Group. By contrast, the mosaic in Room 10, the changing room to the west range baths, belongs to the so-called Saltire Group, also active in the Cotswold region in the course of the fourth century. As its name suggests, its chief distinguishing feature was a preference for using the saltire in the overall layout of the mosaic: the Room 10 mosaic conforms to this perfectly. Some of the motifs, such as the 'pelta-urns' in the arms of the saltire and the split, heart-shaped leaves in the triangular panels, are also very characteristic of this group, as is the extra band of guilloche, seen in Room 10 and on a number of other Saltire Group mosaics.

So the Chedworth villa was patronising mosaicists who were producing some of the largest and most sophisticated mosaics in Britain at that date. Unfortunately, what that date is remains elusive. In general, the dating of the Orpheus Group mosaics clusters around the middle of the fourth century, but so does that of the Saltire Group; therefore, it is perhaps not surprising to find products of both groups adorning the great reconstruction of the west range.

The presence of products of the Orpheus Group in the north wing suggests that the refurbishment of this was broadly contemporary with that of the west range. One north wing mosaic, that in Room 28 which, as noted above, appears to be of inferior craftsmanship, may date to later in the fourth century, partly on the grounds of its workmanship and partly due to its parallels with later fourth-century mosaics at the temple site at Lydney in the Forest of Dean.

Though to us mosaics are hugely important because of their intrinsic interest and because they survive, we must not forget that they were essentially just floor-coverings, albeit rich and expensive ones. Whether the people walking on them would have noticed their designs any more than we would notice the patterns of the carpets or rugs we walk on is a point worth making; only the larger part of the Room 5 mosaic would have been squarely in the field of vision of people at the time, in this case of diners reclining on the couches in the smaller part of Room 5. Other areas of interior decoration, such as the walls, would have been far more 'visible' to people in the fourth century, but sadly we have very little information on them. Excavations at Chedworth have from time to time yielded pieces of wall-plaster painted in various colours, principally a darkish red and a sky blue, both of them common colours in decoration from other villas where the preservation has been better. The most common scheme for Romano-British painted walls was a series of vertical panels divided into three zones. At the bottom was a dado, some 2ft or so deep. Then came the main register, a series of rectangular panels (with their long axis either vertical or horizontal) divided from each other by contrasting borders or by painted architectural framing such as columns; the top zone was a narrow cornice, sometimes painted in imitation of architectural cornices, more often simply horizontal strips of colour. Quite often the dado and main panels were painted in imitation of the coloured marble that was used to veneer walls in the richest and most opulent imperial and senatorial residences, often cut to produce geometric designs and framing (*opus sectile*). Occasionally the centre of the main panels would have a painted *emblema,* a representation of a deity or a human or a scene of some sort, which could be either rectangular or a circular medallion. A small number of sites, including the Great Witcombe villa not far from Chedworth, have also produced evidence for painted ceilings, most often in geometric designs perhaps recalling the coffered ceilings of the richest buildings. The evidence we have, scanty though it is, is that no particular effort was made to coordinate either the designs or the colour schemes of the floor mosaic, the wall paintings and the ceilings of a room. To modern eyes the effect would probably have been overly rich with a clashing series of visual stimuli. But in a way this was the point; the whole purpose was to impress

20. Painted plaster from the Chedworth villa. (*National Trust*)

by the variety and lavishness of the decoration. Conversely, service areas and other parts of the villa which were more workaday may either not have had any decoration beyond a coat of whitewash or wall-plaster painted with the simplest of designs, itself a visual cue to the low status of such a space. From a small number of Roman sites in Britain and on the Continent has come evidence for the exterior of buildings being plastered and whitewashed, sometimes with red painted lines in imitation of the jointing of high-quality ashlar masonry. There is no evidence for this from Chedworth, but this is not proof that it never existed, because such plaster would need regular maintenance and once that maintenance stopped, it would soon fall away from the walls as the villa fell into ruin and it was no longer protected from the effects of frost and weather or repaired when necessary. If the outer faces of the walls of the villa were finished in this manner then this would further enhance the visual effect of the villa, its white walls standing out against the natural colours of the surrounding landscape.

There are two other elements of decoration from the villa, both in stone. One is part of a low parapet or rail consisting of a rectangular panel of back-to-back S shapes either side of a central colonette: where this went originally we do not know. The other is a stone roof finial; from a semi-circular ridge-tile

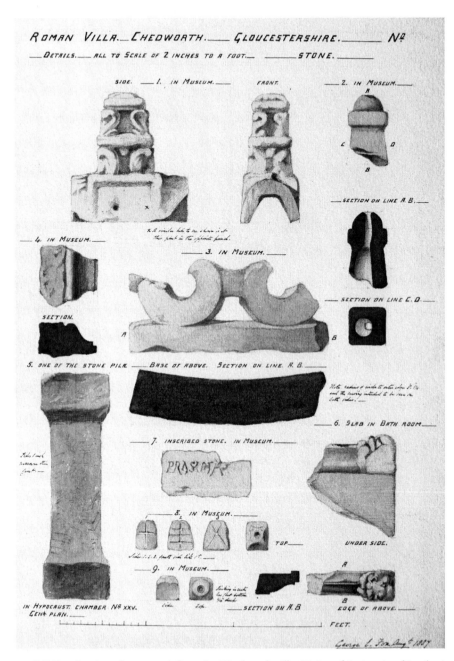

21. G.E. Fox drawing of stonework from the Chedworth villa. (*Society of Antiquaries of London / David Woods*)

rises a rectangular finial in two registers with scroll decoration. This would have enlivened the roof profile of the villa, especially if, as probable, there was a series of these. As well as what one might term the immobile elements of the decoration described above, there were the items of decoration that could be placed into the framing provided by the decorated spaces described above. Besides the representations painted directly onto the walls in fresco technique, we know from classical writers that the Romans also had what we would call pictures, painted representations to be hung on a wall or mounted on an easel or other support. Again, the sources we have for this come from the high aristocracy in the Mediterranean provinces, but there is no reason why such things should not have existed in late Roman Britain. As we shall see in Chapter 5, these could be the occasion for displays of learning on their subject matter.

Sculpture

From Chedworth we have better evidence for a form of art that was clearly very important to late Roman aristocrats, sculpture. The collection from Chedworth consists of a number of pieces all carved in the local oolitic limestone, though originally they may well have had a coating such a gesso which would have smoothed over the stone and been suitable for painting onto. The two most important items were probably parts of two statues of the goddess Diana. The larger consists of the main part of the body, less than life size, with its draperies and a belt running diagonally from the right shoulder suggesting that this was Diana in her personification as huntress, with the strap holding a quiver. Unfortunately we do not know where this was found. The other was found in the original excavation of the site 'behind' Room 5, the dining room, with more being recovered in 1984 to the west of Room 5, which would seem to fit with the idea of 'behind'. The main piece is the base of the statue with the feet, wearing the sort of sandals often associated with Diana; the smaller, 1984 piece was part of the left calf. From the same area came another base with a pair of feet, though whose feet they were we cannot tell, and a third base with a pair of feet is known from the site. Also in the site museum is a fragment of a relief depicting a *Genius Cucullatus*. A *genius* was the presiding spirit of a place, and the *cucullus* was a one-piece hooded cloak, which one can see worn also by the figure of Winter in the dining room mosaic. The *Genii Cucullati* were usually shown as a group of three and were popular in the Cotswolds, with several examples from the area, including Cirencester. Also in the museum is a small relief showing a god recovered from the temple site to the east of the villa (see p. 94). He stands centrally within a niche, holding a hare in his right hand (like Winter in the *triclinium* mosaic) with a hound sitting beside him under the hare. On his left side is a stag. Clearly this is a hunter god, although which one he was is unclear. Silvanus was the most widely depicted hunter god of Roman Britain and the attributes in this sculpture would fit with this identification. But the figure is wearing a 'Phrygian' cap (conical but with a bulging upper part), which in Roman iconography was the sign of something oriental. So this god may have become conflated with an oriental deity such as Orpheus, who is shown wearing this sort of cap on mosaics such as the ones from Woodchester and Barton Farm mentioned above. Such conflation (syncretism) of traits from different deities was very common by the later Roman period. Lastly one may mention a small (60cm-high) niche (*aedicula*) with a shell design at the top, probably to hold a small statue now lost from the building on the ridge above the villa excavated by Farrer which he called 'The Capitol' (see p. 125).

The relatively large and accomplished statue of Diana the huntress suggests another possibility, sculpture as display pieces and thus part of the artistic embellishment of the villa and a reflection of the taste of the *dominus*. Chances of survival have made it clear that some grand villas housed what one might term sculpture galleries. A good example of this is not far away at Woodchester where the excavations at the end of the eighteenth century recovered a concentration of sculpture from one room, including pieces in imported Mediterranean marble. The most spectacular example is that at Chiragan to the south-west of Toulouse in southern France, which had a magnificent set of reliefs of the Labours of Hercules as well as a major series of imperial portrait busts, all in marble. Bearing such instances in mind, one can soon see that many high-class villas in the western part of the Roman Empire have yielded a greater or lesser number of fragments of sculpture, suggesting it was a regular adornment of such establishments. At one level these were statements of wealth by the *dominus*, the more so if a villa in Britain had sculptures in marble imported at great cost and effort from the Mediterranean world. It should also be remembered that such pieces would have been much more visible to the guest or other persons in the villa since they would have been set at eye level, rather than underfoot as were the mosaics. The choice of subject and the scenes represented would also be a statement about the taste of the *dominus* and his command of the artistic and mythological repertoire. It is noticeable that the surviving figures in both the mosaics and the sculpture are drawn from classical Greco-Roman mythology and are, therefore, expressions of the knowledge of these divinities, personalities and myths on the part of the *dominus*, as will be explored further in the next chapter.

Taken all together, the setting of the villa, its manipulation of levels, its lay-out, the types of rooms, their decoration and appointments, make clear that this was more simply than a residence – it was a place to show off the wealth of the *dominus* and to impress on visitors his place within the established hierarchies of power and culture. This chapter has been concerned with the externals of this power and culture, the buildings, fixtures and fittings of the villa. The next chapter will concern itself more with what we may be able to reconstruct of the people, the household and *familia* in the house, and how their social, cultural and religious formation was played out in the fabric of the villa.

FOUR

MEN, WOMEN AND GODS

This chapter will deal with one of the most important aspects of the Chedworth villa but one for which we have hardly any direct evidence from the site itself: the people who lived there and formed the household. What the chapter will do is produce a rather generic picture of what such a household might have looked like by using evidence about the late Roman aristocracy in the western part of the Roman Empire more generally and see how the evidence we have from Chedworth relates to such a picture. Due to the nature of our sources we know far more about the late Roman aristocratic male than we do about the women and children of this class. We know even less about the workers, servants and slaves who formed part of the wider *familia* under the control of the *dominus* (these last will be considered in Chapter 6). It has to be accepted from the outset that this is a speculative exercise, one which is more to do with possibilities, but occasionally probabilities.

To counter the charge that this is entirely an exercise in speculation, we shall investigate how various features of the villa correspond with how such a residence should have looked based on other sources. Much of the chapter will be concerned with the social and cultural attitudes these people held, how they were formed and how they were expressed. One area which will have touched them all deeply was religion, and the fourth century was a time of great change and turbulence as the new, imperially favoured religion of Christianity began to make inroads at the expense of the traditional religions (paganism); turbulence for which we have rare and striking evidence from Chedworth which will be looked at in the latter part of the chapter.

FAMILY AND *FAMILIA*

All historians and archaeologists dealing with late Roman society agree that the family was the most important social unit, providing the 'life support system' for the individual and in large part defining who they were. More difficult to assess is the relative importance of the 'nuclear' and the 'extended' family, but in the ancient written sources it tends to be the nuclear family unit of parents and children, plus close relatives by blood and marriage such as parents and in-laws, that constituted the most frequently encountered family unit; archaeology goes some way to supporting this with excavated dwellings of a size more suitable to this sort of unit than something larger. The extended family was also important, however, through its provision of a wider web of contacts with reciprocal bonds of support. In the Roman world this grouping of people with a shared descent in the male line constituted a *gens*, and at the highest social level such a *gens* could wield a great deal of political power through gaining high office and through its control of many lower-placed people. Familiar examples from earlier in Roman history are *gentes* such as the Iulii (as in Julius Caesar) or the Claudii (as in the Emperor Claudius). Even under the later empire there were still important *gentes* such as the great senatorial dynasty of the Symmachi. Whether there were equivalent 'great families' in provinces such as Britain is difficult to tell due to the lack of evidence, but there is some proof for such *gentes* across the Channel in Gaul, such as the Aviti of central Gaul in the fifth century. If a *gens* stretched through time, at any one moment what mattered was the *familia*, the family by blood and marriage, plus the wider household of dependents, servants and slaves.

What defined the *familia* was that legally all its members were under the control of the senior male, the *paterfamilias*, the father of the *familia*. This control (*patria potestas* − paternal power) over the persons and property of the members of the *familia* was far-reaching; in theory, a *paterfamilias* could exercise the power of life and death over members of the *familia* or even sell his children into slavery. While he lived he had total control over the property of his children and subordinates, who did not even escape his power by marriage;

only when he died did a son in turn become a *paterfamilias*. Evidently, the more extreme powers were seldom exercised and by the fourth century the total power over the *familia* had been to some extent moderated. In return for his powers, the *paterfamilias* was expected to be moral, to bring up his children in the correct way and to perform the necessary religious sacrifices and rituals to preserve the favour of the gods towards his *familia*, particularly in the sphere of the *Lares* and *Penates*, the gods of the household, along with the gods of the *gens*. So the *familia* was more than just a legal unit; it was a cultural and religious grouping. A *paterfamilias* passed his property to his heirs through a will, and could allocate the inheritance as he saw fit. Primogeniture, whereby the eldest son inherited all, was not practised, though the eldest son was seen as the chief heir and became the new *paterfamilias*. If the *paterfamilias* died without making a will, the property was split equally between his children.

Within the *familia* the position of women was, of course, subordinate; nevertheless, they had a certain amount of independent identity. A daughter was subject to her *paterfamilias*; when she married she did not pass under the power of the *paterfamilias* of her new *familia* but remained under her father's *potestas*. This, among other things, meant that any dowry she brought to the marriage did not pass to the new *familia*, since it remained the property of her father; her husband might only enjoy 'usufruct' (use) of the earnings of the dowry. Marriage among the aristocracy, be it senators at Rome or the aristocrats of a province such as Britain, was essentially about uniting two *familiae*, their property and their influence. Such marriages were 'arranged' with little if any regard to the feelings of the man and woman involved, though some clearly did evolve into marriages of affection and respect. Marriage was also about producing children to carry on the line.

In the Roman world, for an adult to be unmarried, particularly for a man, was highly abnormal and socially undesirable; the ideas of celibacy and consecrated virginity being developed by the Christian Church were among the more peculiar innovations of that religion in the eyes of adherents of the traditional religions. To be childless was not only a personal grief but also a social failure of a high order since it meant one's line would die out. Not all marriages succeeded, and until the start of the fourth century either party might divorce the other, and in this case the dowry would revert to the wife's original *familia*. As the fourth century wore on, divorce was made more difficult, but still existed. For a woman, though divorcing her husband might rid her of a man she could not get on with, the risk was that she would lose contact with her children, since they would remain under the paternal power of her *familia* by marriage: access agreements were not a feature of Roman practice. When her father died, an unmarried woman or widow acquired a measure of legal independence; she could, for instance, initiate lawsuits on her own account and could choose whom to marry. Nevertheless, she had to have a legal guardian, usually a male of the *familia*, appointed to act for her in other respects.

The description above is from a Roman perspective, but it must be remembered that the inhabitants of Britain would have had their own family structures, marriage practices and inheritance rules before the Romans arrived. After the conquest of Britain, the Romans did not seek to abrogate these: Roman marriage law and practice would only apply to Roman citizens, so British practices would have continued. But an edict of the Emperor Caracalla (211–218) in 212 gave Roman citizenship to all freeborn inhabitants of the empire. From then on, theoretically at least, Roman marriage law and custom applied to pretty much everyone in Britain, so one could argue that the description above covers late Roman practice in Britain. It is possible, however, that family, marriage and inheritance practice in Roman Britain had been influenced by pre-existing local practice, and it may be that these forms of marriage continued in Britain as provincial variants of 'Roman' marriage. The problem is that we know very little about such practices.

The inhabitants of the province of Britannia are generally characterised today as Celts, meaning they spoke a Celtic language (ancestral to Welsh). Yet what Celtic social structures and practices were are very unclear. The main problem lies with the sources: either they were written from the Greek or Roman side and must lie under suspicion of wanting to tell salacious stories about barbarians (women taking multiple husbands, male homosexuality, sexual freedom of women), as contrasted with civilised Romans, or possibly misunderstanding snippets of information, rather than telling the full story; or if the sources came from the Celtic side, they came from long after the Roman period in Britain, and often from Ireland, which had never been part of the Roman Empire and which by the time the sources were written had been converted to Christianity, thus changing ideas on marriage and the family. Therefore, such sources have to be used very carefully and with a pinch of salt. Nevertheless, the picture is one of nuclear families operating within larger kin-groupings and with common lineages by descent; to a certain extent, not unlike the Roman structures. How marriage operated and the relative positions of adult males, females and children within marriage and the family is almost totally opaque to us. The later sources from Wales and Ireland show that inheritance, as with the Romans, was partible; that is, the inheritance was divided up among the heirs rather than simply passing to the eldest son.

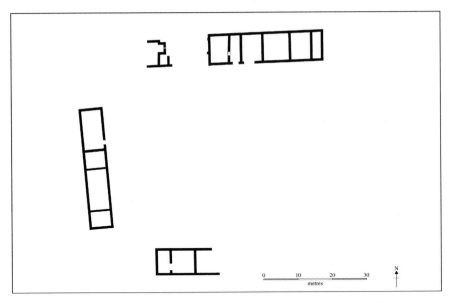

22. Plan of the 'early villa' as 'unit system'. (*Henry Buglass/University of Birmingham*)

This question of partible inheritance has opened up a debate about the way in which some villas in Roman Britain were laid out and this has resulted in a rather different picture of their social structure and thus their layout. Instead of a villa being under the control of a single *paterfamilias* and inhabited by him and his *familia*, the proposal is that a villa was the residence of a kin group, with more than one branch of the same extended family occupying different parts of the complex, the 'unit system'. This proposal came about because some villas seem to have more than one residential building in use at the same time; one example not far from Chedworth is the villa at Spoonley Wood, some 11 km (7 miles) to the north, where as well as the principal residential range there seems to be a lesser one attached to it. The suggestion is that these two units were the residences of a senior and a cadet branch of the same family inheriting in tandem through partible inheritance. Such a scenario has also been proposed for Chedworth, suggesting that the 'early villa' with its separate buildings was laid out according to this social formation and so was the fully developed villa of the fourth century. According to this view, the west range and the north wing each represented a separate residence, with its own bathhouse and dining suite. This scheme of things has not won wide acceptance for three reasons: partly because the number of villas which appear to conform to this pattern is such a tiny minority that they do not offer a firm foundation for a general theory; partly because there are other possible explanations for the duplicate features such as bathhouses; and partly because partible inheritance should presumably lead over time to more than two family units within one complex. So here the discussion will accept that what we are dealing with is an aristocratic household of late Roman type. However, the existence of this debate about multiple family occupancies of villas serves as a useful reminder that we are dealing with possibilities and probabilities, not certainties. Therefore, taking the model of a *familia* under the control of a *paterfamilias*, the *dominus* of the late Roman household, what can we say about the principal actors at a site such as Chedworth, especially the nuclear family of husband, wife and children? It is these people, their upbringing and appearance that we shall look at next.

THE FORMATION OF A *DOMINUS*

The basis of status in Roman society was land and the revenues that came from that land. Entry to the two highest orders of Roman society, the senatorial and the equestrian, was conditional upon property qualifications (as well as the right moral character), as was entry to the *ordo*, the councils that administered the local government areas of the empire. Position was therefore dependent on inherited or acquired wealth. Inherited wealth was the most desirable since with it went noble descent. Wealth acquired through means such as army service or imperial service was acquired in an honourable fashion; wealth acquired through trade was looked down upon. So a man's position in Roman society was traditionally determined by birth, especially if he was born into a landowning family. If born into an established aristocratic family his attitudes to private conduct and public life would be largely formed by education. The sons of the nouveau riche would undergo the same education, being trained into the accepted aristocratic mindset so that the second generation would think and act like their aristocratic friends. An example of this at the highest level is the western Emperor Valentinian I (364–375), who had risen to the purple by military ability and was 'uneducated', sending for the Bordeaux *grammaticus* Ausonius to inculcate in his son Gratian the cultural knowledge and ability and thus the attitudes proper to a high-born Roman. Valentinian knew that what distinguished a member of the upper classes from his inferiors was the fact that he had been educated. Functionally, this allowed him entry to the various professions and occupations where literacy was essential, including the local council, the law and the imperial service; culturally, literacy and the associated knowledge of the classical texts marked him out as a man of the 'right sort', since education was as much about the moral qualities acquired as about the things learnt.

The overall levels of literacy in the Roman world are very difficult to judge, and would have varied enormously by region, class or the occupation of a person; but it is generally agreed that the bulk of the population was illiterate, or had only very partial literacy. Thus, even to be functionally literate – that is, to be able to read and write with ease – was a rare accomplishment and one that could open many doors to social mobility in organisations such as the army, the civil service or the Church. Yet a properly educated man would have been schooled in much more than just his letters. He might have learnt his alphabet in the home, as could happen in a rich household which kept a servant or slave, *pedagogus*, as a sort of 'governor' to the children; then he would have to receive formal training. This might start at a *ludus litterarius*, an elementary school where the basics of literacy and grammar were imparted before moving on to the main stage of his education. Alternatively, he could omit the *ludus* and go straight to a *grammaticus*, a teacher of 'knowledge of speaking correctly' and 'the explication of the poets'. Speaking correctly required knowledge of the parts of speech, how they worked and their relations. Explication of the poets involved detailed examination of the works of the approved canon of writers as examples of the correct use of language, along with the stories they related and the personalities (divine, mythical, human) involved, how they exemplified correct behaviour, plus the religious and philosophical content of the works (see the discussion below under 'Children').

Such education, therefore, was not just a case of developing literacy; it was also an induction into the thought world of the upper classes through imbibing the great poets and the personalities and messages contained in their works. This was what the Romans, borrowing a Greek term, called *paideia*: not just education in our sense of the word, but 'formation', the creation of a man who thought in the approved manner and acted in a moral and virtuous fashion as a result of the precepts on which he had been brought up and in which he had been educated. One way of assessing the standing of an aristocrat in adulthood was his mastery of the literary canon, his ability to come up with an apt quotation, to extemporise a verse, or to 'cap' someone else's quotation; in short, how well he had absorbed his *paideia*. It is clear that many boys did not complete the full education at the hands of the *grammaticus*, but even doing part of that education gave them accomplishments that others lacked. Equally, for most boys the skills inculcated by the *grammaticus* were all they needed, and they would leave his care at the age of about 14 or 15. Only a few would proceed to instruction by an *orator* and the study of rhetoric, which in the Roman world was a skill necessary for influencing political decisions or working in the law courts. By the late Roman period the legal dimension was still hugely important; the political dimension was much more restricted under the imperial system, though addressing the emperor still required formal rhetorical skills, as might appearing before a governor or a council. But it is education at the level of the *grammaticus* that probably is most relevant to us. Roman education may seem to us very limited and stultifying: no breadth, no skills; but its purpose was to perpetuate the limited skills and the body of knowledge required to create a man who had the correct learning and moral attitudes and could behave as a Roman aristocrat. In many ways it was not unlike the classical education in a British public school through much of the nineteenth and twentieth centuries, which itself had similarities to the late Roman system and was also concerned with producing 'gentlemen' with the approved, if limited, knowledge, attainment and moral character, who could still go out and govern the empire.

It has to be said that we have not a shred of direct evidence for the existence of the *grammaticus* in late Roman Britain. We do, however, have a considerable body of indirect evidence in the form of the knowledge of classical culture and the awareness of current fashions and trends among the landowning classes. This is particularly true if we look at fourth-century mosaics in Britain and some other artistic mediums such as silver plate. One of the remarkable features of the mosaics with human and divine figures represented on them is, as has long been noted and commented on, that they show exclusively personages drawn from Greco-Roman religion, mythology and activities, with nothing identifiably drawn from indigenous British or Celtic religion or mythology. Usually this is explained by the desire of the wealthy to show themselves as 'Romanised', as having acquired the trappings of Roman culture. Yet that is to restrict it to a rather superficial knowledge of this culture. A man who had been trained by a *grammaticus* would have internalised a considerable understanding of this classical, literary culture so its expression in art, as on mosaics or plate, could be the result of more personal tastes; the devotion to Greco-Roman subjects would be a reflection of the thought world of these people.

At Chedworth itself we have the Room 5 mosaic of Bacchic/Dionysiac figures, showing a degree of familiarity with the myth cycles involved. In Room 6 there is a mosaic related to those mosaics at Woodchester villa that depict the Greek divinity Orpheus, who was a popular choice for the men who commissioned the mosaics of fourth-century residences in Britain. Other divinities, including Olympian deities such as Jupiter, are also used, along with some more puzzling scenes that seem to betoken knowledge of some quite obscure cults and philosophies. There are also the mosaics that show knowledge of and presumably adherence to Christianity. Finally, one might mention a mosaic from the villa at Low Ham (Somerset) that shows the goddess Venus surrounded by scenes of Dido and Aeneas from Book IV of the *Aeneid* of Virgil (see colour plate 19), one of the canonical texts for study with a *grammaticus*. Divinities such as Orpheus or Christ were important in other parts of the empire, too, showing the awareness of such trends by the Romano-British nobility and of the thought world to which the *grammatici* were the doorkeepers. Even if we have no direct evidence for *grammatici* in Britain, there is circumstantial evidence for their existence. Alternatively, it was not unusual for able or ambitious boys to be sent to recognised centres for such education, which might be at some considerable distance.

For fourth-century Britain the nearest of these major centres was at Bordeaux in south-western Gaul, a region which incidentally had a very flourishing aristocratic villa culture. At Bordeaux they might also have learnt Greek, using the parallel texts, the *Hermeneumata*, mentioned below. Some young Britons would have returned home after their education, but some might have used it and the people they got to know as a stepping stone to careers outside Britain, in areas such as the law, or possibly obtained the patronage to get themselves a position in the imperial service. Patronage was always central to the operation of Roman society, with a more powerful patron obtaining benefits for his clients in return for their loyalty and other services; this was seen as entirely normal and commendable, not at all like the modern world, where it might be viewed with suspicion. One of the most common documents in the later Roman Empire must have been the *littera commendaticia*, the letter of recommendation extolling the qualities of a client or friend and requesting that they be considered for a post. This was one of the services a patron might discharge for a client.

There was also the network of personal friendship and mutual help that permeated the aristocratic world through the bonds of *philia* (friendship). To ask a friend to perform a service, to recommend a friend or client, to put in a good word, all on the strict understanding that one good turn deserved another, was how late Roman aristocratic society worked. To do this there had to be the necessary friendships, and it was probably while under the *grammaticus* that many of these friendships were forged, and those formed at a major centre such as Bordeaux would extend from Britain across Gaul and

Germany and possibly beyond. The bonds of *philia* would, of course, need to be maintained and renewed through correspondence, gifts and services rendered; but it does suggest that the *grammaticus* provided a place to form friendships as well as learn. Even for those who did not venture as far afield as the great centres on the Continent, friendships and links formed at similar establishments in Britain would have been just as valuable at the more local level of aristocratic society.

If the education of a *dominus* was one of the things that marked him out, especially when he spoke or wrote, another important set of messages was conveyed by his appearance and dress. One of the functions of the baths, as we shall see in the next chapter, was to help create the correct bodily appearance of being clean, and either in the baths or elsewhere this would be augmented by the *dominus'* hair being trimmed in the approved manner and his being clean-shaved; if bearded he would have the beard trimmed to the accepted length and in the right style. There are few representations of humans from late Roman Britain, but a valuable find is some wall plaster from a mausoleum at the cemetery of Poundbury outside Dorchester (Dorset), showing a group of men with fairly short hair and full but trimmed beards (see colour plate 20). Portrayals of adult males from the late Roman world overwhelmingly show them with short hair and usually bare-headed. Beards came and went with fashion and personal taste. The emperors of the fourth century were largely clean-shaven, as are most representations of men, but a small number of emperors were bearded, as were some portrayals of men more widely.

The most obvious signal of a man's position in the world was his clothing, visible from a distance with more detailed information closer up. By the fourth century the traditional Roman toga had become a complicated piece of clothing, difficult to wear and keep properly draped and hard to keep clean; it was only used on a limited number of formal occasions, rather like morning dress or white tie today. The normal male dress was the tunic and the cloak, which had long been standard dress for the generality of men (see colour plate 21). It had become widespread among the upper classes as well partly because it was the dress of the army also, which had become hugely powerful and important by this period. The basics were very simple: a tunic that reached down to the knees with sleeves of varying lengths. The sleeve lengths may have reflected social status, with long sleeves being unsuitable for manual work. Tunics were often decorated with two vertical stripes (*clavi*) running down from the shoulders, either all the way to the hem or just partway down the chest and back. These were woven into the tunic and varied from plain to elaborate. Other decorated patches, especially circular ones (*orbi*), were sewn onto the lower part of the tunic. Sometimes tunics were worn with a type of legging. The tunic could be gathered around the waist by a belt. In the late Roman world the belt was an important statement for males, since it was the distinguishing mark of men in the imperial service, either soldiers (the military belt had long been the symbol of a soldier out of armour) or imperial officials (who technically were on military service); therefore, a belt could tell a lot about a man's occupation and status. Over the tunic could be worn a dalmatic, essentially a garment shaped like a T with wide sleeves, again affording opportunities for embellishment and decoration through colour and appliqué patches (the dalmatic survives as the vestment proper to a deacon in the western Church). The outermost garment was a cloak, normally gathered at the right shoulder by a brooch, leaving the right arm free. If these items of clothing constituted standard male dress in the fourth century, the point was how to use them to display the status and authority of a *dominus*. This was largely down to the choice of fabric and the ornamentation of that fabric, along with elements such as belt-fittings and brooches.

Both wools and linens were widely used in the Roman world, and there was a considerable range of quality of the resultant fabric. For the wealthiest people silks were increasingly becoming available, but in Britain it is doubtful that any but the most important men (or their wives) wore silk. The fabrics could have been enhanced by weaving in decoration, either by adjusting the weave to produce twills or satin and other contrasting weaves, or by weaving in threads of a different colour. Finishing such as bleaching would also have marked out the cloth as a more exceptional piece. Dyeing would enhance the effect and might, by the choice of colour, have made a statement about the wearer's job or status (though it would have been prudent to avoid purple, as this was reserved for the emperor; for anyone else to wear it was high treason as it could imply aspiration to the imperial office). Specially woven decorative pieces could have been sewn onto the tunic or cloak to enhance it further. In all these ways the *dominus* could mark himself out by the quality and style of his clothing.

In addition, there would have been the fittings for his belt and brooch. As already noted, the belt could make important statements about a man's relation to the imperial power, by using the buckles, strap-ends and other elements supplied from the state equipment factories, or else aping their design. The metal in which these items were cast was also important; the great majority of the surviving examples are of bronze, but a small number of elaborate and finely wrought gold belt-fittings survive. There is a small, bronze buckle of this type from Chedworth, perhaps from a strap over the shoulder and

23. A dolphin buckle from Chedworth. (*Graham Norrie/University of Birmingham*)

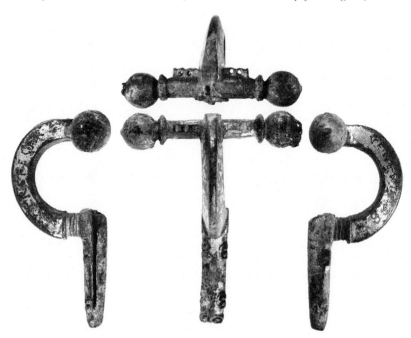

24. A crossbow brooch from Winchester. (*Oxford Archaeology*)

connecting to the belt as in some late Roman depictions. Brooches from the late Roman world were essentially large safety pins designed to hold the cloak together on the right shoulder, rather than the modern meaning of brooch as a piece of jewellery. The most common late Roman brooch was the so-called crossbow brooch. As with the belt-fittings, it was the metal and its decoration that counted. Most surviving examples are in bronze and simply decorated. There are, however, more elaborate types, including hollow-cast bronze brooches that must have been used with light materials and were usually more elaborately decorated with surface gilding, through to the extremely rare gold examples, either solid gold or openwork, sometimes with a reference to the emperor worked into the decoration. These would have been important visual clues about their wearer's status. But it was not just a matter of status: dressing appropriately was another way in which the correct moral qualities of the *dominus* were established; to dress incorrectly or transgressively was a sign of deficient moral attitudes.

THE *DOMINA*

By comparison with her husband, we can say little about the upbringing or formal education, if any, of the lady of the house; this is because the mostly male authors whose writings have come down to us were not concerned with these matters. The role of the upper-class woman, at least as seen by a male-dominated society, was to marry, bear children, run the home and act as a suitable reflection of her husband's position and wealth. Though a woman did not need to be educated in the same way and for the same reasons as a man, nonetheless there is sporadic evidence that girls sometimes acquired literacy (see below), which presumably could help in the running of the house. In the late Roman Empire educated women who could hold their own in conversation were rare and disconcerting (to men at least). Girls were probably married in their late teenage years or a little later to husbands who were a few years older and had been chosen by their parents. Once married the chief duty of the wife was to bear children; above all, male heirs. Given the great dangers of childbirth and high infant mortality, this was a risky business: many women did not survive their child-bearing years and many infants did not make it into adulthood or even childhood.

Of course, the picture was not uniformly bleak. Many couples grew at least to like each other, some even to love. Women did make it into old age and probably outlived their husbands. Children did survive to adulthood, the boys to succeed their fathers, the girls to be married off advantageously in their turn. Yet we have little idea of how an aristocratic woman in a province such as Britain would have passed her days. The picture we have (from male writers of course) of a virtuous woman was that she ran the home, managed the household, looked after the younger children and undertook such seemly female activities as spinning. So at an establishment such as the Chedworth villa she presumably occupied herself largely in running the domestic side of the household so that her husband's and family's needs and comforts were taken care of; overseeing the servants or slaves who staffed the house, and looking after and raising her children. To what extent she would have been able to leave the house and associate with other women of similar social rank is unknowable. Nevertheless, as discussed in the previous chapter, there is no good evidence at a villa such as Chedworth for a women's quarters, so she may not have been secluded from society outside the family, and there is literary evidence that women were allowed a degree of freedom and association with other, similarly placed women.

In public, the wife was essentially a facet of her husband's position. She therefore needed to be attired and to behave in ways that reflected well on him. As with that of the *dominus*, the clothing of the *domina* had changed considerably since the days of the early empire, but similarly the garb, fabric, cut, colour and accessories mattered enormously. By the fourth century Roman women's dress was increasingly styled through cutting and sewing and thus lying closer to the body, rather than being draped over the body as in earlier times. In many ways a woman's clothing was a version of her husband's, consisting of a tunic, with or without leggings, and a *palla* (a mantle or shawl). The tunic seems normally to have had long sleeves and to have extended to the ankles, certainly for higher-class women: an expression of modesty and decorum. As with male clothing, the choice of fabric, its decoration through weaving or dyeing, and its embellishment with embroidered patches all contributed to the overall visual effect (see color plate 22). Sometimes the tunic was gathered with a belt under the bust. Several depictions show women wearing the dalmatic, again functioning as the vehicle for elaborate decorative embellishment, including on occasion fringes. Rather than a cloak fastened at the right shoulder, women used the *palla*, a rectangle of fabric that could be worn in a variety of ways, such as over the shoulders or across the front of the body, and also as a head covering.

Women seem to have covered their heads more than men in the late Roman world, though it seems to have been far from universal. Sometimes they

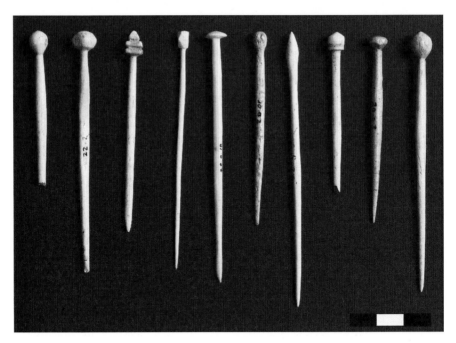

25. Hairpins from Chedworth. (*Graham Norrie/University of Birmingham*)

used a sort of snood, holding the hair in and up as befitted a married or mature woman (only unmarried girls wore their hair loose); at other times it was a simple covering such as the *palla*. There seems to have been no hard and fast rule that women should cover their heads in public, and Roman women do not seem to have been veiled on a regular basis either, though certain contexts such as worship in church are more likely to have involved covering the head. This again suggests that women were not strictly secluded and were allowed to appear in public.

Statues, mosaics, wall paintings and other mediums show a considerable range of hairstyles, with noticeable changes in fashion over time (see colour plate 23). Some made a point of their elaboration, with curls and tresses, sometimes emphasised by jewels and held in place by hairpins in an array of materials, such as bone, jet and various metals, and often decorated (a considerable number of these survive from Chedworth); others were plainer and more severe and depended on elaborate combing, braiding and arrangement of the hair. In either case, these styles could only have been achieved with the help of maidservants to clean, comb and dress the hair; therefore, they were another demonstration of the woman's status and how wealthy her husband was. Alternatively, a similar effect could be arrived at by buying a wig. Conversely, there is evidence that women could be depilated of facial or body hair that did not conform to prevailing notions of feminine beauty, carried out either by plucking or shaving or by the application of unlikely sounding potions.

As well as making the most (or least) of her hair, a woman might wear cosmetics; but for a man to do so was a sign of a distinctly dubious moral character. Cosmetics were designed to do much the same things as they do today: to improve the colour and texture of the face through foundation and powder, to cover blemishes and wrinkles through concealer, and to enhance appearance through such things as rouge, eyeliner or even beauty spots. In addition, there were perfumes, usually made through macerating sweet-smelling substances such as flower petals or spices in light oils. There is evidence for the use of cosmetics and unguents at Chedworth in the form of a small number of the miniature implements used for the preparation and application of cosmetics, plus fragments of the glass vases used to hold preparations and perfumes.

Finally, there was jewellery, for which we have a considerable amount of evidence both from pictorial representation and from hoards of late Roman jewellery discovered in Britain, such as at Hoxne (Suffolk) and Thetford (Norfolk). The preferred metal for jewellery was gold (silver was more common in plate than jewellery) and consisted for the most part of necklaces, bracelets and earrings, sometimes set with semi-precious stones and depending on the intricacy and craftsmanship of the goldsmith for their effect. But for all the elaboration of her clothes, jewellery, hairdo, make-up and perfumes, the *domina* remained essentially an accessory of her husband. She was a mirror for his wealth in that it

26. Small bracelets from Chedworth. (*Graham Norrie/University of Birmingham*)

was he that paid for these accoutrements, and thus she showed off his status and his taste. Dress was also a moral issue: if the *domina* dressed with decorum, richly and yet not too ostentatiously or provocatively, she demonstrated her moral quality and her behaviour as a good wife and *matrona*. Such qualities reflected well on her husband thus further enhancing his moral standing.

CHILDREN

The presence at Chedworth of a small number of objects such as bracelets and finger-rings that would have been too small for an adult to wear (the bracelets have mostly been created by cutting down adult ones) betrays the presence of children, which is hardly a surprise. We know next to nothing about how the children of a well-to-do or aristocratic Romano-British family were brought up in the fourth century. It is likely that the offspring of the richest families, especially the boys, received the sort of education outlined above which would be a necessity for taking their place in society, fitting into the common culture and behaviour of the aristocratic classes. Failing much in the way of direct evidence from Britain, one may turn to a type of document that gives us some insight into the life of upper-class children at this period in the western part of the empire more generally, possibly including Gaul. These are the *Hermeneumata* (Translations – a Latin adaptation of a Greek word), school texts which help with the learning of Greek. They tend to consist of lists of vocabulary and grammatical constructions, followed by sentences in both Latin and Greek. Their purpose was pedagogic: they were there to help Latin-speakers learn Greek; this needs to be borne in mind when reading them. Nevertheless, they are composed in everyday Latin and Greek, not the literary level of these languages, and they use scenes from daily life to familiarise the user with vocabulary, grammar and syntax, rather in the way language courses do nowadays.

Some of the scenes from daily life are written from the viewpoint of children, others of adults. For instance, the first scene is of a child getting up in the morning, washing, dressing (with many words for clothes listed), going out to school with an attendant, then coming home and greeting the household in formal order, starting with father and mother, then other members of the family, the servants and slaves, and ending with the eunuch (and how many of those were there in Roman Britain?). One manuscript gives a very full account of school life. Indeed, it seems to include a description of what went on in a *ludus litterarius* or *schola*, followed by an account of the establishment

27. A schoolroom scene from Neumagen. (*Bridgeman Art Library*)

of a *grammaticus*. Interestingly, girls are mentioned as attending alongside boys, one of the clues that girls might have been educated more than is the picture from other sources. At the *ludus* the exercises consist of reading out loud, writing and grammar exercises, along with some basic mathematics: the three Rs. The passage then moves on to the province of the *grammaticus*, including the learning of Greek. The younger children concentrate on grammar and vocabulary under the tutelage of a *subdoctor*, while the older ones learn with the *grammaticus* himself. They read from the Iliad and the Odyssey of Homer (presumably in Greek), then switch to a list of Latin authors including Cicero, Virgil, Persius, Lucan, Statius, Terence and Sallust. Then it is back to Greek with Theocritus, Thucydides, Demosthenes, Hippocrates, Xenophon and the Cynics. This appears to be a pretty stiff curriculum, but it must be remembered that the *Hermeneumata* are not necessarily accurate depictions of reality and these lists of authors may be about learning the names of the approved Greek writers. It is clear that, as outlined above, the education given by a *grammaticus* was a very narrow and literary one.

Having been released, with praise or blame, from school at the seventh hour (after midday), the child returns home and changes into everyday clothes for a meal, with foods and drinks listed, including *cervisia* (beer), as well as wine. The next section is in the voice of an adult and is to do with the preparation of the main meal. The *dominus* instructs his servants or slaves on the foods and drinks to be served to the expected important guests and travellers, on the spices and condiments to be used and on the preparation of the room, including sprinkling the *stibadium* (dining couch) with petals and perfumes. There is subsequently a section about using the baths, presumably while the meal just ordered is being prepared. It lists the equipment and clothes necessary (one version takes place in a public rather than a private baths, with facilities for exercise but also anxieties about clothes thieves), then the process of bathing, including the use of a strigil (a curved, blade-like implement) to scrape off dirt, and culminates with the bather getting dressed and feeling good about having bathed. Both these sections, since they are written from the perspective of the *dominus*, consist of strings of commands. As has been remarked, much of the day of a late Roman aristocrat must have passed in ordering other people to do things. The descriptions of the main meal itself are, disappointingly, of a simple, sober collation rather than a set-piece formal dinner, after which the diners go to bed. However, one version has the protagonist rolling back drunk after going out for a meal and receiving a sharp scolding (from whom is not known). This version also ends with a section on public life, with a child (presumably a boy) going out to the forum with his father, where he sees a procession of high officials, and they discharge their public and financial business; there are some trials and malefactors undergoing a series of torments and punishments, up to and including the sword used for execution.

It needs to be emphasised once more that this is a schoolbook using scenes from daily life as examples, not an accurate description of what happened every day. The similarities between the various manuscripts suggest there was a certain amount of reuse of standard tropes in the scenes and some of them may have been handed down from earlier versions of the books. Nevertheless, the book does contain a lot of useful and circumstantial information about the sorts of things that could go on: it seems to be related to real life rather than a creation of a fantasy ideal. It equally needs to be emphasised that its applicability to life at Chedworth is probably quite general rather than a direct guide; among other things, the *Hermeneumata* are clearly set in the town rather than the country. In default of better, more direct evidence, they do allow us to contemplate the lot of an aristocratic child of the late Roman period in Britain and how some areas of his life may have been very formally structured.

RELIGIOUS CONTROVERSY

The world of the *Hermeneumata* was a world where the old gods were still reverenced and worshipped, but the fourth century was a time of great religious change and turmoil, and Chedworth has direct evidence for this of a type rare for Britain. At the beginning of the fourth century Britain was still a land firmly devoted to the traditional religions. These are often called by the shorthand of paganism, but this term is avoided here because it suggests there was a single paganism, whereas this was a religious world of great variety and pluralism; also, the term 'pagan' has acquired modern connotations that are not helpful when discussing ancient religions. Therefore, the term 'traditional religions' will be used here, both because it refers to the multiplicity of the religious experience of the people of Britain and because it signals the established place of these beliefs in their lives. During the Roman period in Britain we have evidence for many gods and goddesses worshipped and for places of worship and ritual; we are much less certain about what the beliefs of the individual were or what sorts of worship and rites were performed. Chedworth has evidence for what we see as the two main traditions in the religions of Roman Britain: on the one hand, deities from the Greco-Roman world and from further afield, such as the Olympian gods and goddesses; and on the other hand, British gods and goddesses and other divine beings and spirits. It is the Greco-Roman deities and cults about which we know the most, simply because of the wealth of information about them from outside Britain through which we may assess the evidence from Britain.

From Chedworth itself we have fragments of at least two statues of the goddess Diana, in her guise as the goddess of hunting. It is suggested in the following chapter that the statues of Diana the huntress show the importance of hunting as a recreation at the villa. As well as sculptures, there is the evidence of the mosaic in Room 5, with its depictions of the god Bacchus/Dionysus with Ariadne accompanied by his followers. The myths surrounding Bacchus and Dionysus are hugely complex, but centre on wine, of which they are the gods. Among the myths concerning Dionysus is that he was 'twice-born', though the story has

28. Statue of Diana, the goddess of hunting.
(*Graham Norrie/University of Birmingham*)

29. A sculpture of the god Silvanus.
(*Graham Norrie/University of Birmingham*)

variations as to why and how he was born more than once. The importance of this is that he was of the class of Greco-Roman deities who had overcome death. These deities were worshipped by initiated devotees in what we know as 'mystery' cults: mystery because what went on in them was kept hidden from non-initiates. The common feature is that because the deity had overcome death, he could hold out the promise of rebirth or an afterlife to his followers. Another of these deities was Orpheus, depicted on many fourth-century mosaics in the villas of Britain; and perhaps the best known was Mithras, a saviour-deity who originated in what is now Iran and was particularly followed by soldiers.

Whether the depiction of Bacchus/Dionysus on the floor of the *triclinium* at Chedworth means that the patron who commissioned it was an initiate of the god is very difficult to tell; he might have commissioned it because of the interest in the myths surrounding the god and as a way of showing off his understanding of Greco-Roman culture. Another facet of Roman-style religion is possibly demonstrated by another fragment of sculpture discovered behind the *triclinium* along with the fragments of the statues of Diana. This is a statue-base with two sandalled feet. It has been suggested, though not proved, that the particular style of the sandals shows the statue to be of a *Lar*. The *Lares* were domestic deities that watched over the well-being of the *familia* and its concerns. One of the duties of the *paterfamilias* was to see that the *Lares*, and their companion ancestor deities, the *Penates*, along with the *Genius* (presiding spirit) of the *familia*, were shown due reverence either by himself or on occasion by other members of the household such as the servants. If this base did indeed support a representation of a *Lar*, then that would be another index of the extent to which Roman-style beliefs and practices had been adopted by the aristocracy in late Roman Britain.

30. A statue-base. The original statue was possibly of a *Lar*. (*Graham Norrie/University of Birmingham*)

One other fragment of sculpture is worth noting here: a twice-life-size representation of a human finger in bronze. This must have belonged to an enormous statue of a divinity or emperor. The size suggests that it was probably located in a major temple or in a public space or building in a town such as Cirencester, rather than at a villa. The finger had been hacked off from the statue, suggesting the statue was dismantled, possibly desecrated. The finger then had a square hole punched through its tip, leading to the suggestion that at Chedworth it had been reused as a water spout or tap.

Alongside the evidence for deities derived from the Roman pantheon, there is evidence for deities indigenous to Britain and elsewhere in the north-western provinces. For example, a fragment of limestone sculpture showing what was very probably a *Genius Cucullatus*. A *Genius* was a Roman concept, a spirit who presided over a place, an event, a group of people such as an army unit or a *gens*. This may have mapped easily onto British beliefs in presiding deities and spirits, particularly for natural features. A *cucullus* was an item of clothing common in the north-western provinces, consisting of a long, hooded cloak, like that worn by the figure of Winter on the mosaic in Room 5. The *Genii Cucullati* are deities distinguished by this clothing;

31. Bronze finger from an over-life-size statue, reused as a water spout. (*Graham Norrie/University of Birmingham*)

they are normally depicted in a group of three (an important number in the representation of gods and goddesses in the provinces), as on the delightful sculpture of them from Cirencester, of almost cartoon-like simplicity. Indeed, there is a concentration of sculptures of these figures in the Cotswolds region, though sadly we know next to nothing about what they represented or what their functions were.

Among the more enigmatic religious artefacts from Chedworth are three small limestone blocks, two of which seem to have come from the villa, the third found on the roadside south of the villa. The two from the villa are 18cm (7in) and 16cm (6½in) high, that from the roadside 8cm (3¼in) high, and all three are roughly in the form of a miniature Roman altar. The tallest has a crude outline figure with two dots for the eyes and five dots arranged in a quincunx (as with the five on a die), interpreted as representing the nipples, the navel and the testicles, and he is holding what appear to be a spear and a shield. Above the figure is scratched a short text that may identify him as the god Lenus Mars. Lenus was a native god known from the Moselle valley in Germany where he seems to have had healing properties; his assimilation with the Roman god Mars suggests he also had warlike qualities – this identification with Roman gods is often the only way to know the name and character (or an aspect of the character) of indigenous gods and goddesses.

Why he was being worshipped (if indeed he was the inscription is very difficult to read) at Chedworth is unknown. The other two altars simply bear
incised geometric designs. What the function of these miniature altars was is
not certain. They seem to be scaled-down versions of a votive altar. This was
an altar erected in discharge of a vow made to a deity; a thank-offering to
the god/goddess who had granted a person his wish. These altars therefore
reflect the often contractual nature of Roman religion as it sought to maintain the favour of the gods.

There are two religious buildings associated with the site of Chedworth
that are worth noting. Some 900m (half a mile) south-east of the villa, on the
slopes overlooking the Coln, lay what was probably a temple; not a temple
of the type familiar from Rome itself, but rather a type typical of the north-
west provinces and usually consisting of a square or rectangular (more rarely
circular or polygonal) structure with a smaller, taller room of the same shape at
its centre. Explored in the 1860s and again in the 1920s, it seems to have been
of the square within a square type. It was probably from this temple that the
sculpture of the god Silvanus with a dog and a stag now kept at the villa came.
Originally an Italian god of fields and woodlands, in Britain Silvanus seems to
have become more of a god of hunting, with dedications to him in this guise
from a number of places in Britain, especially in the area of Hadrian's Wall. The
other religious building was the shrine over the spring in the north-west angle
of the villa complex itself. In classical Roman religious practice this would have
been a *nymphaeum*, a shrine to the nymph(s) who presided over the spring; we
saw in the previous chapter how the layout of the west range and the north
wing was specifically adapted to frame the *nymphaeum*. The local religions very
probably had gods or goddesses or presiding spirits at such places, so here the
imported and indigenous cult practices may well have overlapped to a considerable extent. The spring was, of course, the source of water for a range of
functions in the villa, but this way the water and its uses were placed under the
care and blessing of the nymphs and the spring was at once useful and sacred.

It is the *nymphaeum* that provides us with the clearest evidence for the religious turmoil that was to become such a part of the Roman Empire and its
peoples in the fourth century; at this time, the religion of Christianity was gaining imperial support and rose to become the dominant religion of the empire,
increasingly seeking to suppress and supplant the traditional religions. Until the
start of the fourth century we have little reliable evidence for the presence of
Christianity in Roman Britain. At that time, Christianity was at its strongest
in the eastern Mediterranean provinces of the empire and was also undergoing its worst-ever persecution at the hands of the eastern Emperor Diocletian

32. Small altars from the temple near Chedworth. (*Graham Norrie/ University of Birmingham*)

33. Excavations at the temple in the 1920s. (*Bristol & Gloucestershire Archaeological Society*)

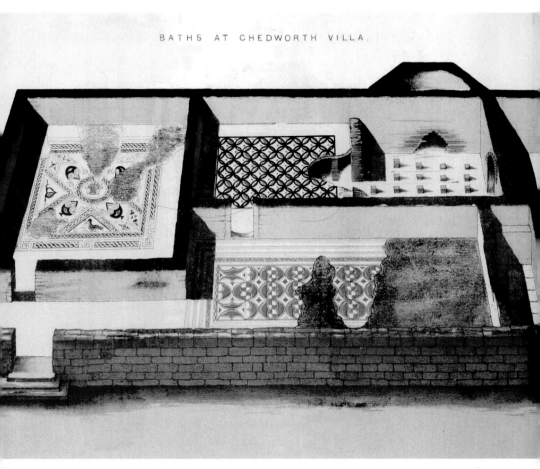

BATHS AT CHEDWORTH VILLA.

1. 'Roman Villa at Chedworth', by J.W. Grover (1868), an engraving of the west baths. (*British Library*)

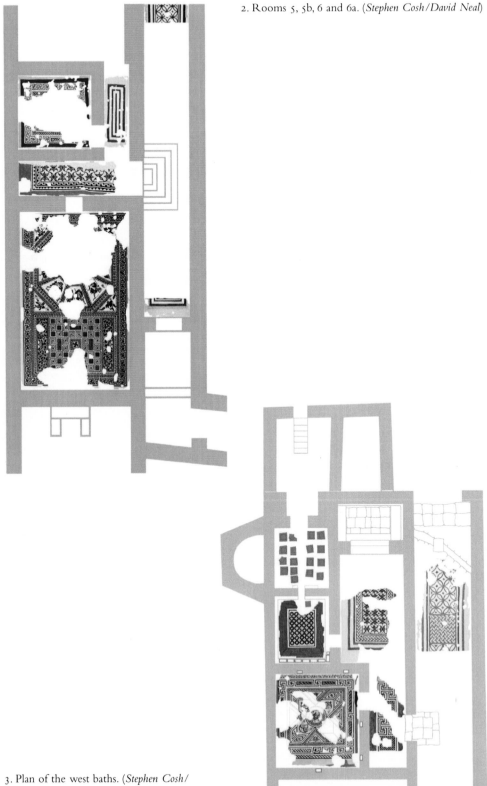

2. Rooms 5, 5b, 6 and 6a. (*Stephen Cosh/David Neal*)

3. Plan of the west baths. (*Stephen Cosh/ David Neal*)

4. Rooms 11 and 12 in the west baths. (*Ian Shaw/National Trust*)

5. The reception Rooms 24 and 25. (*Simon Esmonde Cleary*)

6. Reconstruction of the latrine by Tony Kerins. (*National Trust*)

7. The *nymphaeum*. (*Simon Esmonde Cleary*)

8. A reconstruction of the *nymphaeum* by Tony Kerins. (*National Trust*)

9. Reconstruction of the villa from the south-east by Tony Kerins. (*National Trust*)

10. The west gallery from the south. (*National Trust / Guy Salkeld*)

11. An aerial view of Great Witcombe. (*www.webaviation.co.uk*)

12. View from the *nymphaeum* over the inner courtyard with the museum and shooting lodge. (*Simon Esmonde Cleary*)

13. The west gallery mosaic. (*National Trust*)

14. The Room 6 mosaic. (*National Trust*)

15. The Room 10 mosaic. (*Stephen Cosh & David Neal*)

16. The smaller part of the Room 5 mosaic. (*Luigi Thompson*)

17. The larger part of the Room 5 mosaic. (*Luigi Thompson*)

18. The figure of Winter from Room 5. (*National Trust Images / Ian Shaw*)

19. The mosaic with scenes of Dido and Aeneas from Vergil's *Aeneid*, at Low Ham villa, Somerset. (*Taunton Museum*)

20. Wall plaster showing a group of men, from a mausoleum in the fourth-century AD cemetery at Poundbury, Dorchester. (*Dorchester Museum*)

21. Silistra (Bulgaria) tomb painting of a fourth-century official and his wife. (*Andrew Poulter*)

22. A pepper pot in the form of a richly attired woman from Hoxne, Suffolk. (*British Museum*)

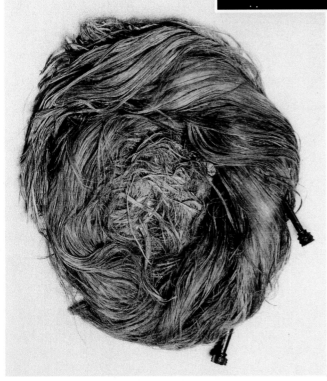

23. A preserved head of late Roman hair with jet hair pins, from York Museums Trust. (*York Museum*)

24. Reconstruction of the north baths by Tony Kerins. (*National Trust*)

25. The 'Banquet of Mnemosyne' mosaic showing women dining. (*Bridgeman Art Library*)

26. Reconstruction painting of Roman Cirencester. (*Corinium Museum*)

27. John Scott, 3rd Earl of Eldon (1845–1926) by Thomas Price Downes. (*The Bridgeman Art Library*)

28. The Heritage Lottery Fund cover-building. (*National Trust*)

(284–305); his western colleague Maximian (285–305) seems to have concentrated his persecutions in North Africa, perhaps because Christians were at their strongest there as compared with other areas such as Gaul and Britain. In 306 Maximian's successor, Constantius I, died at York and his son Constantine, who had been at his father's deathbed, had himself illegally proclaimed emperor by the army there. Six years later, on the eve of the battle for Rome itself, Constantine had a vision of the Christian symbol and a promise that in this symbol he would conquer. For the rest of his long reign (306–337) Constantine favoured the Christian Church, being baptised on his deathbed.

All Constantine's successors, with a couple of short-lived and unimportant exceptions, were Christian, and by the end of the fourth century the practice of traditional religions had been outlawed, their shrines and temples closed and Christianity was well on the way to becoming the near-universal religion of the empire. To have the backing of the emperor completely changed the fortunes of Christianity, giving it the most important support and encouragement it could obtain in the Roman world. However, this was not achieved without a great deal of resistance and on occasion bloodshed (Christian against Christian, as well as Christian against adherents of the traditional religions). A problem in understanding what went on stems from modern writings often presenting the process as the unstoppable rise of Christianity at the expense of the traditional religions; in fact, it must have been a far more messy process with as many successes and reverses for Christianity as for the traditional religions, especially in an area like Britain where Christianity appears to have started from a position of considerable weakness.

34. Chi-rho on a coping-slab from the *nymphaeum* at Chedworth. (*Graham Norrie/University of Birmingham*)

We have a record of a delegation of Christian bishops from Britain at a Church council at Arles in southern Gaul in 314. These may have been the bishops from the capitals of the four provinces into which Britain was by then divided, but if so, Cirencester is not mentioned. Cirencester would have been the natural seat for any bishop of the area since it was the principal town of the *civitas* of the Dobunni. There are other mentions of bishops from Britain later in the century; nevertheless, Britain does not seem to have been an island that was strongly evangelised during that century. A small number of buildings have been identified as Christian churches, but these identifications are not certain. The finding in 1981 of a hoard of silver objects with Christian symbols in the Roman town of Water Newton (Cambridgeshire) would certainly seem to attest to a Christian community. A small number of villas have evidence for Christianity, such as the wall painting from Lullingstone (Kent) or the mosaic floor at Hinton St Mary (Dorset). But overall, the amount of evidence for Christianity is not impressive, and suggests it mainly made headway among the upper classes; to be cynical, some people probably jumped on the imperial religious bandwagon. By contrast, there is a great deal of evidence that the traditional religions were still observed and their places of worship open and functioning down to the end of the fourth century. By concentrating on the evidence for Christianity we are perhaps neglecting the bigger picture of religious life and practice in late Roman Britain.

Nevertheless, Chedworth does give us a glimpse of these controversies and the changing fortunes of the religions. This is at the *nymphaeum*. Of course, a *nymphaeum* was by definition a building dedicated to the traditional religions, with its veneration of water nymphs; and since, as we have seen, the spring was central to the existence of the villa its nymphs were powerful personalities within the religious landscape and life of the villa and its community. At some date, presumably in the fourth century, three of the stones that form the surround to the octagonal basin of the *nymphaeum* had the Christian chi-rho symbol carved into them: one very competently, the other two more crudely. The chi-rho was the standard Christian symbol of the late Roman period before the cross came into more general use. It consisted of the first two letters of the Greek word *Christos*, chi (CH) and rho (R), which to us look like X and P respectively, superimposed on to one another.

Carving this into the slabs would seem to be a deliberate attempt to impart a Christian significance to the *nymphaeum*, replacing its traditional vocation. It has been suggested that this could have represented the conversion of the *nymphaeum* into a Christian baptistery, since at this date baptism was administered to adults standing in a basin such as this, rather than to infants.

However, this is unlikely, since in the late Roman Church baptism was administered by bishops and known baptisteries (on the Continent) are associated with the bishop's main church, which by Church law had to be in the chief town of his see. Moreover, a baptistery was a subordinate element of the bishop's church and all the excavated examples of this date elsewhere in the empire are associated with such a church. Chedworth was a villa out in the countryside and there is no evidence of a church building at the site with which any baptistery could be associated. Nevertheless, it is clear that at some stage the *nymphaeum* was Christianised and it is not unreasonable to argue that this meant the *dominus*, and presumably his immediate family, had converted to the new, imperially approved religion.

What adds a further twist to the tale is that these slabs were themselves found removed from the *nymphaeum* and reused as building stones. It would seem that their Christian meaning was no longer important. It is unlikely that Christians would behave so casually towards the central symbol of their religion, so possibly the owners of Chedworth reverted back to the traditional religions. Also at the *nymphaeum* a pagan altar (without any inscription, unfortunately) was at some stage buried in the north-eastern corner of the building. Whether this was to remove the trace of the old gods when the building was Christianised, or whether it was put there for safe keeping when the *nymphaeum* was no longer used, we cannot now tell.

This evidence from Chedworth is echoed not far away at Cirencester, presumably the seat of any bishop of the Dobunni in the fourth century. There, according to an inscription discovered in 1891, one Lucius Septimius ——, governor (*rector*) of the province of Britannia Prima, restored a statue and a column erected under the old religion (*prisca religio*), dedicating the inscription to Jupiter Best and Greatest. Lucius Septimius (because of later damage to the stone we do not have his full name) was a native of Reims in northeastern Gaul and clearly a devotee of the traditional religions. Why the statue and column needed restoring is not explicitly stated, but the reference to them being dedicated under the 'old religion' suggests that the 'new religion' – Christianity – was a force to be reckoned with; however, whether Christians had vandalised the monument or whether it had just fallen into disrepair under the new religion can only be conjectured.

A bit further away, at Bath, is another index of the rise of the new religion in this region. Throughout the Roman period suppliants had deposited into the waters of the hot spring lead tablets with incised writing, calling down the vengeance of the presiding goddess of the spring, Sulis (Minerva), on suspected malefactors. Usually this was because of theft, and the tablets requested

35. The *prisca religio* inscription in Cirencester. (*Corinium Museum*)

painful punishments upon the thief until they restored the stolen property. Sometimes a tablet gave named suspects. If not, catch-all categories were given such as 'whether man or woman, boy or girl, slave or free'. Interestingly, one tablet adds *seu christianus seu gentilis* (whether Christian or gentile), showing Christians to be numerous enough and sufficiently distinctive to be worth a specific mention. So Chedworth and its region have yielded a number of pieces of evidence that allow us to see that the struggle between the old and the new religions, for which we have such eloquent evidence elsewhere in the empire, was taking place in Britain and in the Cotswold area, too.

One other inscription from Chedworth is worth mentioning for the light it may shed on wider concerns. The 1864 excavations turned up a building stone with a roughly cut text. The poor quality of the original lettering

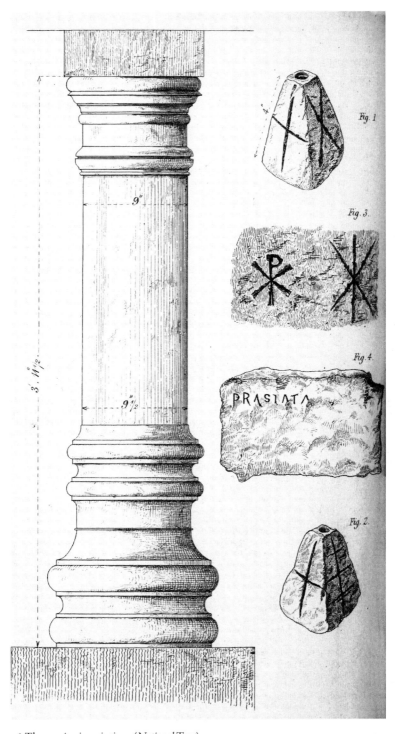

36. The *prasina* inscription. (*National Trust*)

combined with subsequent damage has left it difficult to read (originally it was read as PRASIATA – see p. 172), but the most probable reading is *PRASINA*, a Latin word for 'green'. This was also the word for one of the chariot-racing factions at Rome and elsewhere that were distinguished by their colours: Reds, Whites, Blues, and Greens, rather in the way that major football teams today are referred to by their colours. Like modern football teams they also had huge, committed followings and rivalries between the factions sometimes spilt over into violence and even riots. By the fourth century, the Reds and Whites had become overshadowed by the Blues and Greens, which had developed into more than just sporting teams, and at Rome and later Constantinople had taken on political importance. The chariot and other races in the circuses or hippodromes had long been major sporting events, and circuses were constructed at many of the most important cities in the empire. By the fourth century, circuses were also an integral part of major imperial residences, such as the one at Trier in the Moselle valley, where the emperor appeared in person before his subjects. Until recently, the Chedworth inscription was one of the few pieces of evidence for an interest in circus sports in Roman Britain, but the discovery from 2005 of such a circus at Colchester has shown that this could have been more than a theoretical interest. The Chedworth text, therefore, links the villa into a major sporting-cum-political axis in the late Roman world.

As stated at the outset, much of what it is outlined in this chapter is based more on evidence of practices from elsewhere in the western provinces of the Roman Empire than in Britain. What really underpins it is consideration of the ways in which the social structure and the thought world of the late Roman aristocracy in a villa might have been created and operated. The chapter has been concerned with the education that formed such aristocrats, particularly the menfolk, and the ways in which it instilled not just practical skills, such as reading and writing, but also moral precepts and values. It has also looked at the changes brought about by the growing influence of Christianity, a religion that because of its greatly increased prominence and power had to consider its own ideas on matters such as family life or education. As was also stated, there is not a great deal of direct evidence for this from Chedworth itself. Nevertheless, there are snippets of information – ranging from the choice of mosaic subjects to hairpins to developments at the *nymphaeum* to the single word *prasina* – to sustain the argument that the *dominus* and *familia* at Chedworth were aware of and participated in the wider currents of intellectual, social and religious life that characterised the fourth-century west of the Roman Empire. If we accept these currents as framing the lives of these persons, then a number of significant aspects of the villa can be explained in ways that make sense and which it might not otherwise have been possible to elucidate. In the next chapter we shall look at how some of these attitudes were played out, particularly in the sphere of entertaining honoured guests whom the *dominus* wished to impress through the quality of the entertainments he laid on for them.

FIVE

COMPETITIVE
ENTERTAINING

The bonds of friendship and mutual regard and obligation, *philia*, outlined in the last chapter, and the reciprocal obligations of patron and client were central to the functioning of aristocratic society in the Roman world, and no more so than in the fourth century. Who you knew and who knew you were of paramount importance, and a late Roman aristocrat would see to it that these bonds were maintained and strengthened through correspondence, gifts and services rendered either directly to his friend or patron or on behalf of one of their clients or dependents. Perhaps the most formal and most personal way in which such bonds could be reaffirmed was by entertaining a friend or patron, allowing the lavishness of the entertainment to express the degree of regard in which they were held and providing the face-to-face contact that was the most effective way of getting things done. Various elements went into making up a suitable entertainment, but of these there are three that are constant and which will be looked at here since they combine ostensibly simple activities with a complex social code and set of expectations (and thus also the possibility of things going horribly wrong); these are hunting, bathing and dining.

HUNTING

As in many societies before and since, late Roman hunting was a ritualised aristocratic pastime whose social meanings were far more important than any nutritional gain to be derived from the kill. There is a certain amount of evidence from the Chedworth villa that supports the idea that hunting was carried out from it. On the one hand, among the surviving finds are a number of arrowheads and spearheads of varying sizes and types. Legally, hunting was one of the only reasons why a civilian might carry weapons, but this was a law dating back some 400 years to the time of Julius Caesar and whether it was enforced or observed in fourth-century Roman Britain is far from certain. Nevertheless, the presence of a number of weapons suitable for the hunt is worth noting here. There are also the two statues of Diana, one in her guise as the huntress, and the statuette of the hunter god Silvanus from the temple near the villa, again suggesting that hunting was important. The most direct evidence from Chedworth is the considerable quantity of antlers recovered from the excavations in the lower south wing; clearly some of these stag hunts had been successful. These antlers were not used as trophies but had been sawn up as the raw material for objects (discussed further in Chapter 6). Also, analysis of the animal bones from the 2000–01 excavations on the upper courtyard showed that some of those that at first sight were of domestic pig

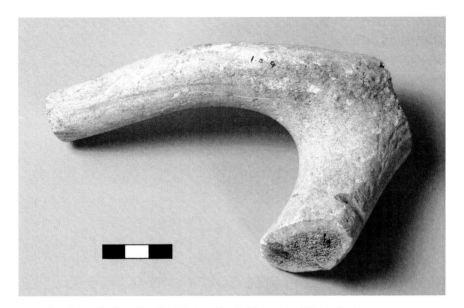

37. Antlers from Chedworth villa. (*Graham Norrie/University of Birmingham*)

38. Projectile heads from Chedworth villa. (*Graham Norrie/University of Birmingham*)

were in fact of wild boar, which can only have been at the villa because the boar had been hunted.

Late Roman hunting primarily concerned land animals, though we also know that hawking was an aristocratic pastime and presumably the quarry would often be other birds so there may also have been wildfowling. Small game such as hares was hunted, but it was hunting the larger and more dangerous animals that was the real measure of a huntsman's prowess. The favoured animals for the hunt were deer and boar, boars of course being a very dangerous quarry and one of the ultimate tests of the hunter. The strength and skill required to close in on and kill a trapped and frightened animal of great size and strength was a supreme demonstration of the bravery and manly qualities of the hunter, and thus for an aristocrat of his nobility and *virtus*, a word deriving from the root *vir* (man), thereby meaning something rather different to the related English word 'virtue'.

A Roman hunt was conducted in ways unlike modern fox or stag hunting, since the basic aim was to drive the animal(s) into a net or netted area where they could be despatched. To lay on the opportunity for a friend or patron to demonstrate his *virtus* in this way was to pay him a considerable compliment. And of course hunting was not a cheap pastime. A *dominus* would have to ensure that his estates contained the right sorts of conditions for the animals to live in, mainly wooded areas, so this would constitute a specialised area of landscape use. In the Middle Ages and later there were forests, parks and chases set aside mainly for hunting. We have no direct evidence of this for Roman Britain, but it is a possibility well worth bearing in mind. Then a supply of the appropriate animals would have to be assured through long-term breeding, and presumably protection from poachers. The hunters would require hounds, again a matter of long-term breeding and training, presumably by specialist staff. Ancient sources comment on the different qualities of different types of hound and their use against different types of prey.

The actual hunt would require a certain amount of equipment, such as the nets, as well as the servants to set them up and to act as beaters on foot or on horseback to put up the animals and drive them towards the nets and the hunters. However, over and above the actual episodes of chasing and despatching the quarry, hunting acted as the frame for more leisurely social interaction. By the fourth century, there are literary references to and artistic depictions of highly formalised meals or picnics (perhaps a rather too informal term) taking place within a day's hunting. The hunters, richly clad, are depicted reclining on a semicircular couch covered with cushions and shaded by temporary hangings and awnings. They are being waited on by well-dressed servants and being served food and wine; sometimes movable vessels for heating the food or drink are shown. Clearly this was a setting that required a considerable degree of forethought and preparation in the provision of the furnishings, the staff and the victuals. We shall be looking at the formalities of dining in more detail below, but this was an open-air variant of the formal banquet and therefore as much of an opportunity for displaying wealth and taste and for talking to guests as was its indoor cousin.

To judge by the incidence of literary references and artistic representations, the importance of hunting both as a pastime and as a formalised social event seems to have increased in the third and fourth centuries. It is repeatedly depicted in art. Perhaps the most spectacular example of this is at the villa of Piazza Armerina in central Sicily, where one mosaic entirely devoted to depictions of the hunt floors a corridor 70m (230ft) long and another floors a room and has a depiction of a hunt meal. A similar depiction is on the central medallion of a huge silver dish probably found in the Balkans and dedicated to a certain Seuso. It shows the diners under an awning and above them scenes of the hunt. The rim of the dish is decorated with a series of scenes of hunts of a variety of animals, from the more usual stags to the unusual and dangerous bears or lions and leopards; bears might have been hunted in Roman Britain, lions and leopards presumably not. Hunting scenes were also popular on the most expensive of aristocratic sarcophagi from the later second century on. As well as these high-cost and high-status mediums for the depiction of hunts, they also occur on much less costly and more widespread objects, such as engraved glass bowls, pottery or even the handles of folding knives, showing a hound attacking a hare for example. One of the more delightful inscriptions from Roman Britain was set up in the second century by the commander of an army unit in what is now County Durham, giving thanks to Silvanus for letting him take a remarkably fine boar that none of his predecessors had managed to kill. Therefore, the hunt as an important pastime had wide currency and it would seem certain, both from general principles but more particularly from some of the finds, that it was practised from the Chedworth villa.

BATHING

Hunting seems to have been an activity that started early in the morning and lasted through into the afternoon. Upon their return, one can see that the hunters would be weary, saddle-sore and perhaps hurt, and their destination, at least for the *dominus* and his guests, seems to have been the bathhouse to wash away the grime and the aches and pains. Even if they had not been out hunting the baths were an important place not only for the obvious purpose of getting clean, but also for creating the right appearance; and they also functioned as a social area. The principle of Roman baths was simple and corresponds to what was termed the 'Turkish' bath in nineteenth- and twentieth-century Britain (ultimately, the Turkish bath derived from the late Roman bathing practice in the Levant mediated to the Turks through the Islamic *hammam*).

Having divested themselves of their clothing and been anointed with oils, the bather passed through a cold room (*frigidarium*) to a warm room (*tepidarium*) where they warmed up and began to perspire; then they entered the hot room (*caldarium*) which was filled with steam either from basins of water heated by the hypocaust beneath them or by special boilers placed over the hypocaust furnace (large iron supporting beams for such a boiler were found in the north baths at Chedworth). In this atmosphere perspiration would increase, opening the pores to clean out accumulated dirt. At this point, if a bather had a companion or servant they might be scraped down with a strigil to remove any sweat, dirt and oils, and might have a plunge in the hot pool to clean off the last of the dirt. They would then return to the *frigidarium* and take a plunge in the cold pool to tone the body. This fulfilled the basic function of cleansing. Variants on this form of bathing include the provision of rooms of hot, dry heat (*laconicum*, similar to a sauna), or a room more specifically designed to promote sweating (*sudatorium*).

Bathing in the Roman world had long been linked with exercise. This normally and sensibly preceded the bathing, but was also part of producing a suitably fit body, so was closely connected to ideas of how a person with the leisure to bathe and take exercise should look and feel physically. In the most lavish public bathing complexes there was also provision for cultivating the mind as well as the body in the form of libraries, discussions and recitals (*mens sana in corpore sano* – a healthy mind in a healthy body – in the words of the Roman poet Juvenal). Major public complexes might also have hairdressers and barbers so that bathers could keep their hair in the current fashion (men as well as women), and men could be clean-shaven or bearded according to the dictates of fashion; if bearded, the beard could be properly styled and at some periods depilation was fashionable.

The bather would smell sweeter if scented oils or other preparations had been used, so the sense of smell as well as sight was engaged. Bathing was, therefore, much to do with producing an appearance that was 'Roman', according to current tastes – one reason why baths were so widespread in the Roman world and hardly existed outside the frontiers in Europe, where dwelt barbarians who were defined to the inhabitants of the empire as much by their unkempt look as by anything else. Bathing was practised by both men and women, but contrary to the more fervid imaginings of novelists the two sexes hardly ever bathed together, and when they did, at least in public baths, it was the occasion for disapproving comment. The most likely ways of providing for both sexes were either to have separate facilities for men and women, or that men and women should use the same facilities but at different times, and there is evidence for both of these. This was at public establishments, though considerations of sexual modesty and the segregation of and chaste behaviour in women probably meant private bathhouses would function in a similar way (see colour plate 24).

The Chedworth villa was unusual in that it had two sets of baths, apparently in operation at the same time, at the north end of the west range and the west end of the north wing, thus separated only by a short distance. Their basic plan and structure was considered in Chapter 2, but here we should look at how they were used. The first thing to note is that these are not 'public' baths in the same way as the large complexes at towns such as Cirencester, let alone the great imperial baths of Rome and other major cities. By the fourth century, these major public baths seem to have been falling out of use, perhaps in part due to the cost of maintaining their structure after 200 years or so and the cost of firing and servicing them, but perhaps also because of the rise of private baths, particularly at aristocratic residences. These latter, of course, allowed bathing in a much more exclusive environment, exclusive both in its basic sense of shutting out other people, the hoi polloi, and in the sense of bathing with companions of similar high status.

Both of the Chedworth bathhouses were originally of the Turkish type, though the baths in the north wing were probably later converted to the hot, dry *laconicum* regime. Why the villa had two sets of baths and so close together is not clear; the wear on the stylobate, the base stones, of the colonnade of Room 20 on the direct line between the two bath suites suggests that not only were they in use at the same time, but were even used together. One possibility is that they were originally separate suites for men and women, but it is only a possibility. The wear in Room 20 might result from the conversion of the north baths to a *laconicum* so that the two bathhouses became part of one circuit of bathing.

To take the example of the better-preserved baths in the west range: though they are small, a deal of care and money had been lavished on them. Obviously the construction of equipment such as the hypocausts, the wall flues and the vaults, as well as the pools and basins and connecting up the water supply and providing drains (still visible cutting across the west gallery mosaic), was a specialist job. Most of the rooms were floored in mosaic, and the baths lined with smooth, limestone slabs. There is evidence that the walls were painted and some at least of the ceilings took the form of barrel vaults; the apsidal plunge pool (Room 13) of the hot room might well have had a semi-dome. On entering this bathhouse the user would be struck not only by the warmth and the steamy atmosphere, but through the steam would be visible the colours of the mosaics and the painted walls (and ceilings, probably), decorating a series of intimate but architecturally sophisticated spaces.

The north baths are less well preserved, but they also were floored in mosaic, they also have a sequence of semicircular pools which might have been covered by semi-domes, and in the final phase with the new plunge pool on the northern side with the two smaller side pools separated by a low wall with dwarf columns, there was again a measure of architectural sophistication. In these intimate spaces a limited number of people could bathe at the same time, so for men it would be the perfect setting in which to relax and wash the cares of the day away in the company of friends, guests and patrons with whom one could at the same time discuss business or politics in confidence. There are ancient references to slaves or servants being present at such times with trays of drinks or 'nibbles'. The women of the house and their guests could equally relax in the baths and discuss their cares and concerns, probably in an appropriately gendered fashion. Not being public baths there is no sign of a formal exercise area, but the mid-fifth-century writer Sidonius Apollinaris from central Gaul, when describing his or other aristocrats' villas in his letters, often mentions ball games and alludes to dice and board games. Late in his career Sidonius Apollinaris became bishop of Clermont-Ferrand, so it is perhaps worth saying a word about the attitude of Christianity to baths.

Christianity, or more importantly Christians, had developed in a Roman culture to which bathing was central; one way in which Christians were discriminated against was to ban them from the public baths. Not surprisingly, therefore, we find baths provided at major complexes such as bishops' residences, so the Church was not against bathing as such. Nevertheless, theologians and moralists increasingly viewed bathing as problematic. On the one hand, there were occasions when they recognised it as beneficial to the faithful, especially for medicinal or therapeutic purposes. On the other hand, they came to disapprove of bathing for bathing's sake since it sought to pamper rather than to discipline the body and might give rise to lascivious thoughts or behaviour. Such scruples do not appear to have troubled the inhabitants of the Chedworth villa in the fourth century; indeed, the baths were a prominent architectural and social component of the villa.

DINING

Cleaned, relaxed, shaved or coiffed and properly attired, hosts and guests would be prepared for the last and possibly most fraught entertainment of the day: the formal dinner. This was played out to a complex set of rules about setting and behaviour and was codified within a rigid set of social expectations. As much as this was an opportunity for the host to show off his house, his servants, his food and drink, his entertainments and his taste, so too was it a chance for him to commit the sorts of social or cultural faux pas that would diminish him in the eyes of those he wished to impress.

At Chedworth, the largest room in the west range, Room 5, has long been identified as the dining room, with the kitchen, Room 3, not far away in the south wing; Room 5a has been acknowledged as the area for stoking the furnace that heated the hypocaust under Room 5, and Rooms 5b and 6 were lobbies or reception rooms leading from the west range gallery into Room 5 itself. Room 5, as was seen in Chapter 2, was divided into two unequal parts and floored with the most lavish and highest quality mosaic to have survived from the villa. It was also suggested that Room 32 at the east end of the north wing was another dining room, perhaps a summer dining room or possibly a women's dining room, with Room 30 as the kitchen and Rooms 31 and 31a being the lobbies and entry space equivalent to Rooms 5b and 6. As will be seen, in terms of the theatre of late Roman aristocratic dining, this configuration makes good sense.

Formal dinners seem to have started late in the afternoon towards sunset. Generally, the participants seem to have been men, though there are some late Roman representations of banquets where women are shown banqueting separately or as participants, sometimes reclining along with the menfolk, sometimes sitting in an impressive chair, the continuation of a long-established practice. Therefore, although women were probably not always present at banquets as participants, they could on occasion be (see colour plate 25).

Under the early empire the diners had reclined on couches, usually three of them arranged round three sides of a room and giving rise to the name for the room, the *triclinium*, from 'three couches'. This arrangement did continue on to the later empire, but was increasingly replaced by an alternative arrangement. This took the form of a semicircular couch with cushions, particularly a large bolster along the inner edge of the couch. The couch was known either as a *stibadium* from the Greek for cushions, *stibades*, or as a *sigma*, referring to the C shape of the couch seen from above, resembling the form at the time of the Greek letter *sigma*. The hollow of the curve was occupied by a table. What other furniture, if any, there was in the room is uncertain. It is possible that there was a type of display case or set of shelves known as an *abacus* (presumably because the rectangular frame and shelves reminded people of the counting device) on which silver plate or other items of value might be displayed. At Chedworth in Room 5, the couches or *stibadium* would have stood in the smaller part of the room, on the part of the mosaic simply decorated with geometric designs, leaving the larger and more ambitious mosaic with

Bacchic/Dionysiac themes in the larger part of the room unencumbered and visible to the diners (see colour plates 16, 17).

The two parts of the room were separated by stub walls; these could have supported columns in turn supporting either an arch or a flat entablature to give an architectural frame to the dining area and the diners, rather like a modern proscenium stage. What there was in the way of wall paintings and whether there was a flat or vaulted ceiling we cannot now know, but these could have been areas that contributed to impressing guests. If the meal did start towards the end of daylight, then the Room 5 dining room would have had to be lit by artificial light, since the sun would already have disappeared behind the ridge to the west of the villa. If Room 32 was a dining room, it would have stayed lighter for longer, perhaps supporting the argument that it was a summer dining room. An important difference between Rooms 5 and 32 is that Room 5 was totally enclosed and the focus was on the diners in the smaller part of the room; with Room 32 it is likely that there was as much importance accorded to the diners looking out of the room as to the diners being looked at. For both rooms, lighting was probably provided by stands holding lamps or candles. The latter are much more likely, since lamps are rarely recovered from late Roman sites in Britain. Beeswax or tallow candles could have been made from local resources; beeswax candles would of course smell sweeter and would demonstrate more clearly the host's wealth, particularly if large numbers were provided. By placing the candelabra to light certain areas, such as the *stibadium* and the diners, and to leave others poorly lit, a considerable theatrical effect could have been created.

A formal Roman dinner unrolled according to a set pattern and there were numerous points along the way where judgements could be made on the lavishness and taste (or otherwise) of the host's provision. The guests would be greeted on arrival by slaves, some of whom would be bearing trays of food or cups and flagons for serving wine; others would have basins of water and towels for the guests to wash their hands – these are sometimes shown with flowers or garlands for the guests. Paintings and mosaics showing these servants suggest this may have been a stage before the meal proper; at Chedworth, were anterooms such as Rooms 6 (see colour plate 2) and 31 the setting for this formal reception?

The servants themselves could be a luxury item, though whether they were slaves or free at a villa such as Chedworth we cannot tell. Most depictions of them show young males, though sometimes young females also. They were often richly dressed in embroidered tunics and the elaborate ways in which their hair was dressed led to them being called *capillati* or *crinati*, 'the ones with the hair'. One way in which male servants' hair was dressed in the fourth century was like the modern 'page boy' haircut, but with a longer tail of hair down the back of the neck. This is a style used in Roman depictions of Germanic youths and warriors, therefore dressing servants' hair in this way may have been a sort of conceit, as if the guests were being served by pet barbarians. Literary references make it clear that the servants who poured the wine were particularly prized and shown off; a good-looking, graceful, well-dressed boy in this role was a real ornament. Some texts strongly suggest that these servants might be expected to pander to guests in other ways once the meal was over. Once the meal proper began the servants had a variety of specialised tasks to perform. Some were responsible for serving and clearing the food, others for keeping the diners' glasses or goblets charged, and others for bearing the basins of water and towels needed for diners who were using their fingers, aided by a knife to cut up the larger pieces of food and spoons for serving and eating. The diners themselves would, of course, be elaborately dressed in rich tunics, possibly with an over-garment such as a dalmatic; such clothes would combine elegance and display with practicality.

The diners reclined on the couch of the *triclinium* or *stibadium*. To us this seems an uncomfortable pose well suited to promoting indigestion, but it distinguished rich and aristocratic diners from their social inferiors, who would have sat on chairs or benches at a table to eat: as so often comfort was sacrificed to make a social point. Who sat where was very carefully arranged to show distinctions of status and honour. If we imagine looking towards a *stibadium* couch, the host lay at the left-hand end, the guest of honour at the right-hand end, and the other guests in order of precedence from beside the guest of honour, round the curve of the couch, with the most junior guest next to the host. Obviously, selecting the order of precedence was laden with the possibility of giving offence: how to place a member of an old-established, landowning family in relation to a parvenu imperial official or army officer or indeed one of those new-fangled Christian bishops?

The food, its variety, preparation and presentation, was central to the effect created by the dinner. Our evidence comes on the one hand from pictorial representations and on the other, more prosaically, from food remains excavated at sites such as Chedworth. An attentive host would make sure that there was a variety of foods served; some would come from his own estates to show the range and quality of his products, but he would also ensure that a gamut of exotic foods was placed before the diners, such as preserved foodstuffs from a distance or the herbs and spices with which they were preserved. For a site such as Chedworth, the harvest of the seas and rivers could also be brought to the table, such as fish, shellfish and the oysters for which Britain was reputed.

In the later Roman period great emphasis was placed on the ingenuity of the preparation and cooking of the food, the use of spices, contrasting flavours like sweet and sour dishes today, and combining different ingredients and tastes. Much of the evidence for this comes from the late fourth- or fifth-century 'cookbook' usually associated with the name of the early imperial Roman gourmet Apicius. Though many of the recipes are clearly practicable, there is a certain amount of debate as to what extent some of the more elaborate, and to us implausible, recipes were really intended for the kitchen and how much they were designed to impress the reader without actually being put into practice; or, as in the case of the recipe involving flamingo, were entirely about ostentation rather than nutrition. Other evidence is again pictorial, from mosaics and paintings depicting banquets. From these one gets some sense of the actual sequence of dishes.

Dinners do not seem to have been served in the way with which we are familiar: the way known in the nineteenth century as 'Russian service', where the same dish was presented to all the diners at the same time as a course in the meal. The Roman system seems to have been more akin to 'French service', where a large number of different dishes were placed on the table at once, possibly in two or three 'removes'; perhaps an equivalent modern experience is the Chinese banquet. It is likely that there was some system like 'removes' with the meal starting with a selection of light dishes, along the lines of our hors d'oeuvres, before moving on to more substantial cooked meats, poultry and fish, before concluding with sweetmeats. However, even in such an apparently simple system there were social pitfalls lurking. From the comments of a second-century writer it would appear that each 'remove' of dishes was not a free-for-all – there was an etiquette as to which dishes should be eaten in which order (shades of modern worries over the order of use of cutlery) – and he advises the inexperienced to watch what other diners do and follow their example. Presumably there was also the etiquette of offering particularly desirable morsels to other guests, sharing dishes or letting the guest of honour have first choice; equally, presumably, there was scope for bad manners by diving in for favourite dishes and using long arms and sharp elbows. The end result of such meals is shown by the popular mosaic subject in the Mediterranean provinces (we do not yet have one from Britain), the *asaroton* ('unswept'), depicting a floor at the closing of such a meal littered with pieces of food.

The accompanying drink was as important as the food, and we have already noted the high status of the wine waiters. Wine seems to have been the civilised drink, and the Roman world had clear notions of the relative

tastes and merits of wines from different geographical areas and of differing vintages. There is some evidence for viticulture in Roman Britain itself,
though what the wines were like and how widely they were distributed we
do not know. Our best evidence for the importation of Mediterranean and
other wines into Britain comes in the form of amphorae, the thick-walled
ceramic containers with two handles used for the bulk movement of liquids
such as wine, olive oil and fish sauce (*garum*). Unfortunately for us, by the late
Roman period the use of amphorae, which survive well in the archaeological record, seems to have declined in favour of perishable containers such as
barrels or wineskins, which survive only rarely. There are, nevertheless, some
Mediterranean wine amphorae known from late Roman Britain and it may
be that wine was imported from Gaul in tuns. Certainly we have the equipment from late Roman Britain for the correct serving and consumption of
wine as well as of food.

If our vision of how food and drink were prepared and eaten depends
almost exclusively on evidence from outside Britain, particularly the
Mediterranean, the same is not true of the vessels in and on which it was
served. For reasons we still do not understand, Britain has produced the
largest and richest concentration of late Roman silver plate from the entire
empire, with a marked focus in East Anglia with hoards such as Mildenhall
and Hoxne, both in Suffolk. These contained vessels related to eating, ranging from large dishes the better part of 1m (3ft) in diameter, to smaller dishes,
bowls and platters. Other hoards from Britain and the Continent contained
flagons and strainers for the service of wine along with goblets and cups for its
consumption. Many of these pieces were highly decorated with relief scenes
from the traditional mythologies and occasionally from the new, Christian
stories. Others had more restrained, geometric decoration, some of which
was enhanced with gilding, or with niello, a silver sulphide giving a black
inlay. Detailed examination of some items show evidence of cut marks and
other marks suggesting they were used to eat off, even if any hot food would
quickly go cold; again, ostentation trumped practicality. Yet many pieces,
including some of the largest and most extravagant, such as the huge, elaborately decorated 'Oceanus' dish from the Mildenhall treasure, show little or
no sign of use. They could conceivably have served as trays on which to put
other, smaller serving dishes, or for fruit, but perhaps most likely they were
simply display pieces, laid on the table to impress or ranged on furniture such
as the *abacus* display stand. Literary sources make it clear that the most lavish
plate of all was of gold, but perhaps not surprisingly none of this has come
down to us from antiquity, although quite a quantity of silver has.

39. Glass bowl with a hunting scene from Wint Hill villa, Somerset. (*Ashmolean Museum*)

As well as precious metal dishes and vessels, it is clear that by the fourth century glass was a widespread material, particularly for drinking vessels, and some of it could be exceedingly costly and elaborate. Roman glass was made with soda and over time an impressive degree of mastery of colour and thickness had been achieved, with colours ranging from the completely transparent to blues and greens, reds and yellows, all made possible by the addition of the right chemicals at the molten stage. Most vessels for serving and consuming liquids were formed by blowing, either free blowing or blowing into a mould, often giving the effect of embossed designs such as a bunch of grapes.

40. Oceanus' dish from the Mildenhall treasure. (*British Museum*)

Vessels could be left plain or embellished with incised decoration, sometimes figured, such as the bowl with a hunting scene from Wint Hill illustrated above. The most spectacular and elaborate examples of drinking vessels were the so-called 'cage cups', carved from a solid block of glass, leaving the cup surrounded by a 'cage' of openwork glass attached to it by a series of struts which the glassmaker left as he carved between the cup and the cage. Sometimes different parts of the cage were fashioned in different coloured glasses.

The skill and time required for a highly trained craftsman to execute such a piece is hard to imagine; such pieces must have been as costly as silver if not gold. Not surprisingly, fragments of such vessels are rarely found in Britain, but a huge range of vessels in coloured and incised glass is known from fourth-century sites. The effect of this glass would be further enhanced by the colours of the liquids they contained, such as wines, and whether they were viewed by direct or transmitted light. The dining table would have been dressed with fine linens and napery and a variety of costly dishes and cups in a range of materials and colours to produce a startling visual effect, probably heightened by the changing quality of the candlelight in the room.

The physical setting, the servants, the food and drink were crucial elements in the provision of a lavish and successful dinner. So also were the conversation and the interaction between the guests. To give a flavour of this, we may turn to an account of dinner recorded in a letter by the mid-fifth-century Gallic aristocrat Sidonius Apollinaris. This dinner took place at Rome and was hosted by the emperor himself, Majorian (457–461); for Sidonius to be invited was a signal of honour, but dinner with the emperor brought its own dangers. Sidonius explains the seating in terms of the order of precedence of the guests; as most junior he found himself next to the emperor. With the meal well advanced Majorian took control of the conversation, engaging the guests in strict order of seniority (one guest is angered by being passed over and forgets his manners), with a combination of compliment, questions and literary topics, with approbation for quick wit. When Sidonius' turn came the conversation had moved on to the dangerous subject of satire and the emperor taxed Sidonius with writing satirical broadsheets. In order to defend himself Sidonius asked for the emperor's permission to write satire and in return had to produce a verse on the spot, which he did, having gained time to think by summoning a servant so he could wash and wipe his hands: the impromptu verse gained loud applause.

This account shows the formal structure of the conversation, with the host leading and addressing his guests in order of precedence (though dinner with the emperor would probably be more formal and tense than with most other hosts). Clearly, knowledge of literature and quick wit were required, and Sidonius' ability to extemporise verse stood him in good stead. Here we see the product of the formal education discussed in the last chapter, in particular the emphasis on knowledge of verse forms and of the common, approved literary canon. This was not an after-dinner conversation in our somewhat unbuttoned sense, but rather a serious social contest with places gained or lost through the ability to deploy the fruits of such an education. Of course, we only have Sidonius' version of events, suitably polished up for an epistle that was itself a highly developed literary form, but the general context of an aristocratic dinner and of the agonistic conversation ring true. This is by no means to claim that a dinner party at Chedworth would have proceeded with quite the same level of political and personal threat, but that there could have been some sort of formal conversation displaying the cultural assumptions and virtuosity of the host and guests seems very plausible.

For the most highly educated who wished to show off their learning and rhetorical style to their guests, there was the *ekphrasis*. This was a highly stylised disquisition about a work of art or an event or other topic. It was designed to show the speaker's mastery of classical mythology, its personalities and stories, possibly by giving novel interpretations of them, and also his command of rhetorical form, of correct Latin usage and of the poetry he would have studied under the *grammaticus* – possibly also the more advanced skills of formal rhetoric – combining all these in a virtuoso display of style and content (or at least so he hoped). How much this would have happened among the provincial aristocrats of late Roman Britain is very much open to question, but in the context of the Chedworth villa we might point to the mosaic of the larger part of Room 5, showing Bacchic/Dionysiac themes. Passively, the choice of subject matter would be appreciated by educated guests; actively, it could be used as the prompt for such displays of verbal dexterity, as might any pictures or other representations in the room, such as decorated plate.

At the end of the formal part of the meal the host might provide entertainments of a less cerebral and taxing kind. We have literary reference to and artistic depictions of entertainers, such as musicians and dancers, who would presumably, at Chedworth, have performed in the larger part of Room 5, thus using the figured part of the mosaic for something distinctly less high-minded than an *ekphrasis*.

It must be acknowledged that again the picture presented above is one that is almost entirely derived from sources outside Britain and it could be objected that its direct relevance to Chedworth is limited. This is an objection that has force, but there are reasons for thinking that the picture is not that misleading. The most important evidence is that of the physical remains of the two dining suites, above all Room 5 and its mosaic. Their layout conforms very closely to dining rooms in other parts of the Roman Empire, even if they are not at the top end of the architectural scale. The division into two unequal parts, the dais in Room 32 and the plain and figured areas of the mosaic in Room 5, all correspond with practice elsewhere. These rooms would have provided the correct sort of framing for dinners of the type outlined above and it is difficult to think of any other likely use for such rooms. If we admit the likelihood that Rooms 5 and 32 were of this type, then the rest follows. That is not to say that it follows exactly in all the details we have seen above, but the general form and structure of the dinner would have been recognisable to visitors from elsewhere (otherwise the host would be accounted a failure). The assembled company would certainly not have been the emperor and senior courtiers, but questions of precedence and placement would have occupied the diners as much as they did Sidonius in Rome a century later. The diners would surely have been formally received and served according to the style of late Roman Britain. The food might well have been very different from the sorts of luxury items we have in the pages of Apicius, but the host would still have been concerned to put on a show through the quality of the ingredients, their preparation and presentation and the quality and presentation of the drink.

Archaeological remains such as animal bones, showing which meats were favoured and how they were butchered, and the preserved remains of the seeds of herbs and spices can give us some idea of the range of ingredients used and the possible flavours, but not how they were put together in detail. Recent research on the archaeological evidence for eating and drinking in late Roman Britain has shown that there was a wide range of foodstuffs available and a degree of regional variation in these; therefore, a late Roman banquet in Britain might well have looked and tasted very different to its Italian or North African equivalent. Likewise, such dinners would have been the setting for formal and informal conversation, possibly including the more rhetorical essays to demonstrate the learning and culture of the host. If what went on at such a dinner in fourth-century Roman Britain differed in several respects from practices elsewhere, then this was a reflection of regional practices and places in the social and cultural hierarchies. The sort of formal late Roman dining discussed above gives us a framework for understanding the physical layout of parts of the Chedworth villa and for thinking about the types of things that went on in those spaces, but for which we do not have the direct evidence from Chedworth.

Therefore, if we understand, at least at a general level, some of the uses to which the villa might have been put as a place where its owner could show off to guests his wealth, his taste in its appointments and fittings, his servants, his cooks, his entertainments, and provide for the thrill of the chase, then we go some considerable way to understanding why the Chedworth villa contained the rooms and suites it did and why it was laid out and decorated the way it was. It was a means whereby the *dominus* could display his standing in society and reinforce the bonds of *philia* and patronage by which so much of the late Roman aristocratic world was ordered.

SIX

THE VILLA IN
THE LANDSCAPE

The preceding chapters have taken as their focus the visible remains of and other evidence from the site of the Chedworth villa, the residential complex. But this did not exist in isolation. The villa was set within a particular landscape; it depended upon the economic basis provided by land. The surpluses mobilised from that land had to be converted into money or goods and services. The villa was only one of a large number in the region giving a wider social, cultural and economic setting, and that regional grouping of villas was itself one of a limited number of such groupings across Britain and the western empire. So to understand the villa it is necessary to look more widely in order to understand why it was the way it was. It is the purpose of this chapter to set the Chedworth villa within these wider contexts, starting with a tight focus around the villa itself then progressively widening the field of view.

THE VILLA IN ITS IMMEDIATE SETTING

The modern visitor to the villa gets an impression that it was in a very secluded spot, cut off from the wider world, nestling in its combe and closely surrounded by woodland insulating it from the countryside around. This is a misleading impression, one very much created by the woodland of the Stowell estate coming close down to the small area owned by the National Trust. There is good evidence that in the fourth century the villa sat within a landscape marked by its presence. Excavations since the 1970s have demonstrated that there were dependencies of the villa to the north-west and south, outside the main ranges of buildings but servicing the villa. To the north there was a wall upslope of the north wing, probably partly to prevent soil washing downhill. It also defined an area from which the hypocausts in the wing were fired and presumably where wood was stacked and maybe other supplies moved out of sight. A similar area seems to have existed outside the west range where a wall ran west from the outside of its angle with the south wing, then returned north, creating a defined space. What went on south of the south wing we do not know because of the modern track and car park, but there was a door through the south wall from the kitchen, leading into a small passage giving access to this area as well as to the latrine. Therefore, the immediate vicinity of the villa was probably given over to service areas tucked away out of sight of the principal suites of rooms.

In the woodland surrounding the villa today are two Roman monuments, most likely to have been linked to the villa and whose presence argues strongly for a much more open landscape for them to have been visible. In 1864, as part of his work on the villa, James Farrer uncovered a separate building 155m (170yds) to the north-west of the villa and on the ridge overlooking the combe and the surrounding countryside. He christened this The Capitol. His description of it is summary and not easy to understand, but it seems to have consisted of several small rooms and in it was found a stone niche with a scallop-shell decoration in its head.

41. The scallop-headed niche. (*Graham Norrie / University of Birmingham*)

The structure was later destroyed by the construction of the railway (see p. 175). Given its position, this was a structure designed to be seen. The scallop-headed niche is of a type sometimes found in association with funerary monuments, so it is tempting to think of The Capitol as a mausoleum; perhaps this was how the family asserted and made visible their and their forebears' ownership of the land and position in the locality, but this is speculation.

The other monument in the vicinity of the villa is better known; this is the temple-style building 640m (700yds) east-south-east of the villa on the slopes overlooking the Coln. This was also initially explored by Farrer in 1864, but explored again more thoroughly by St Clair Baddeley (see p. 182) in 1925–26 after the acquisition of the villa by the National Trust. Though badly pre-served and difficult to access because of trees, it was possible to show that the structure consisted of stone walls enclosing a near-square 12.5m (41ft) by 12m (39ft 6in) internally. At the south-western angle some large, well-cut, ashlar masonry remained *in situ* on the foundations. The plan resembles that of the most common type of Romano-British temple or shrine, a square within a square or a rectangle within a rectangle (less often concentric circles or concentric polygons). Such a plan is usually reconstructed as a taller inner chamber where the cult statue or other focus of devotion stood, surrounded by a lower ambulatory or walkway. The Chedworth example consists only of a single square: some temples to this design are known; alternatively, it may be that the evidence for another chamber did not survive.

The 1920s excavations recovered a number of fragments of short, plain stone columns which presumably would have decorated the building. The north side of the building faced out over the Coln valley and may have been the entrance facade. Just inside the centre of the north wall was found a shal-low pit containing the antlers of a red deer. This building is said to have been where the stone relief showing a hunter god with a dog and hare, probably the deity Silvanus (see p. 94), was found; possibly also the two incised representa-tions of warrior figures on small, simple altars. So, one possible interpretation of the building is that it was a temple to this hunter god, again emphasising the importance of hunting at Chedworth. Another possibility is raised by the fact that both Farrer in the 1860s and St Clair Baddeley sixty years later found fragments of human bone. Normally, this would be a highly unusual find at a Roman-period temple site since human remains brought ritual pollution that would have defiled the sanctuary. However, there is a small group of sites from Roman Britain where the architectural form of this type of temple has been borrowed to act as a mausoleum. It is possible that rather than a temple in the normal sense, this building was a temple-mausoleum. In this case it would

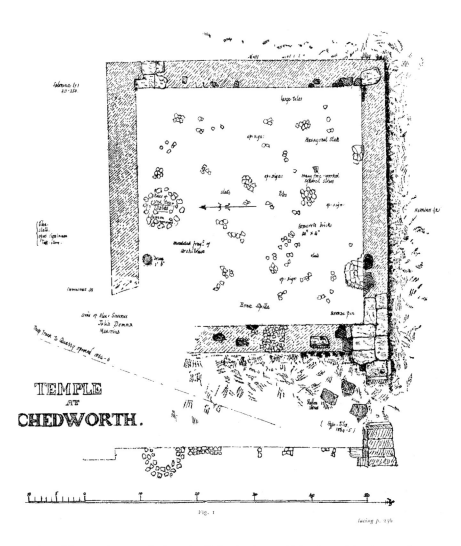

42. Plan of the temple near Chedworth villa by St Clair Baddeley. (*Bristol & Gloucestershire Archaeological Society*)

be difficult to explain the relief of Silvanus and the deer antlers. Like The Capitol, this building, whatever its precise function, was clearly positioned to be seen by people travelling along the floor of the valley either to the villa or to other destinations.

It should also be noted that the 1860s excavations brought to light pieces of hypocaust flue tile and other building material from the vicinity of the temple, and that Farrer noted visible walls and other remains in the woods 183m

(200yds) upslope to the south of the temple; there may, therefore, have been a settlement associated with it. One lesson from the possible funerary functions of The Capitol and/or the temple is that though we currently know a fair amount about life at the Chedworth villa, we know nothing about death and burial. We do not know the locations of any proven burial, cemetery or mausoleum, yet such there must have been, and they would have been a very particular type of land use in the vicinity of the villa. The other lesson both of The Capitol and of the temple or mausoleum is that the landscape immediately around the villa may have been marked by buildings and monuments related to the villa and which imposed the visible presence of the villa and its owners further afield than just the combe in which the villa lay. Much of this land could have been in the ownership of the *dominus*, and it was on this land that ultimately the wealth of the owner and the means to build and maintain the villa depended.

VILLA, ESTATE & ECONOMY

The fundamental meaning of the Latin word *villa* is a farm or rural property; the modern archaeological use of the term to signify a rural establishment in the Roman architectural style, while a useful shorthand, does obscure the basic importance of its being a rural, agriculturally productive entity. All the cultural and social values physically embodied in the remains of the Chedworth villa that we have looked at already rested ultimately on the villa buildings and their inhabitants being supported by an economically viable estate, producing the surpluses that could be expended on the creation and maintenance of the villa and on the lives and lifestyles of its people. The problem is that we have very little direct evidence that allows us to reconstruct this estate, its activities and the people who lived and worked on it: the best we can do is to outline the possibilities and to use what evidence there is to see where it points.

We shall start with the very word 'estate': to us it tends to imply a single body of land surrounding the 'estate centre' rather like in the modern world, for instance the Stowell estate. There is warrant for this from Roman texts, none of them unfortunately referring directly to fourth-century Britain, though some, such as the writings of Ausonius or Sidonius Apollinaris, refer to fourth- and fifth-century Gaul, which may not be too far off the mark. What these two writers, and many other aristocratic late Roman writers, also show is that an estate might consist of different parcels of land in the same province, or an aristocrat might own several estates with one principal one, or in the case of the grandest aristocrats they might own estates scattered across the empire. Any particular villa might, therefore, represent the income from a variety of properties in a variety of places, not simply a single property surrounding the villa. If this were the case for the Chedworth villa, it is possible that there was some sort of 'home farm' in order to supply the household with foodstuffs and other commodities; it is likely that Chedworth conformed to the pattern seen at other Romano-British villas where the excavations have been sufficiently extensive to show agricultural dependencies (sometimes called the *pars rustica*) near the residential buildings (sometimes called the *pars urbana*). At Chedworth the obvious place for this is the lower courtyard which Farrer left unexcavated, but the 1997 excavations on the lower part of the south wing mentioned in Chapter 2 suggested that this part of the complex too was residential. So it may be that the agricultural dependencies were separate from the residential complx, which is the part we have.

At a number of larger and richer Romano-British villas we can observe a separation between the agricultural and the residential parts by means of a wall or other demarcation; at Chedworth the cross-gallery separates the garden from the lower court. As with so many Victorian and other early excavations on villas the focus was on finding the main residence with its mosaics, hypocausts and baths; the excavators were simply not as interested in the rest of the villa complex. In consequence, at Chedworth we do not have the buildings such as barns, store buildings or animal byres, or the finds from them such as ploughs or agricultural equipment like the Roman version of the combine harvester, the *vallus*. Nor indeed do we have the buildings that housed the estate workers, responsible for the sowing, raising and harvesting of crops, the care of the flocks and herds, the preservation of the woodlands, and the making and maintenance of the necessary equipment. This means that we can say very little about their social and legal status. In the late Roman world more generally there weas a series of gradations of social and legal dependency on a *dominus*. Some pople involved with the villa may have been 'free', that is they were not legally under the control of the *dominus*. They may have been tenants, working estate lands in return for rent, either in coin or in the form of produce, rather as tenent farmers might today. Or they could have been 'free' but part of the direct labour force of the estate, living and working on it and receiving lodging and food, perhaps also with the possibility of earning some money from their own animals of gardens. Such people may have held the legal status of *colonus*, a person who though technically 'free' (not a slave) was tied to the land and worked it for a *dominus* to whom he (or she) paid rent (not unlike a medieval serf). A *colonus* was not allowed to leave the land without permission, and if the land was sold the *coloni* attached to it would pass under the control of the new proprietor. Whether there were slaves on an estate such as Chedworth in the fourth century is a question which on current evidence cannot be answered. Slavery was famously a feature of the Roman world, in particular Rome and Italy in the late centuries BC and the early centuries AD But it would be extremely unwise to assume that this held good for the rest of the empire at all times. In fact, there is very little direct evidence for slavery in Roman Britain, and that mainly comes from the first and second centuries and is particularly associated with the army. So it would be wisest at present to say that there could well have been slaves at a villa such as Chedworth, but that there is no proof positive and so we have no way of telling how important a component of the workforce they may have been. As well as any slaves working the estate, it could also well have been the case that some of the household servants were slaves rather than free, since late Roman sources from outside Britain (such as the *Hermeneumata* looked at in Chapter 4) regularly refer to slaves in aristocratic households. So it may be that some of the workforce lived in buildings attached to the villa itself; it may be that some of them lived in separate holdings at a distance from the villa. Others might hold part of the estate in leasehold and pay rent in cash or in kind. Such legal and tenurial relationships are next to impossible to derive from archaeological evidence.

On the more positive side, there is some evidence from the various excavations on the villa for what was being produced on the landholdings attached to the villa, particularly from the more recent excavations in the first decade of the twenty-first century. This evidence takes the form of carbonised grain and animal bones. In the 2000–01 excavations on the upper court, and thus dating to the fourth century, a small amount of carbonised grain was recovered, mostly of the simple form of wheat, emmer (*triticum dicoccum*), with possibly some spelt wheat (*triticum spelta*), which was the wheat most commonly grown in Roman Britain. Barley, another common crop in Roman Britain, was also present. There were some fragments of nutshell as well, but too small to be identified to a species. In the lower south wing, the very late (probably fifth-century) pit dug into the gallery contained some burnt grain. Again, the principal components were emmer wheat and barley, along with a single grain each of oat and rye, the latter two also well known in Roman Britain. The presence in both areas of emmer wheat is a little surprising, since compared with spelt wheat it did not give as heavy a yield of grain. It is also worth noting that a large millstone was recovered in 1864 from Room 30, showing that grain was being processed on a very considerable scale.

43. Millstone found in Room 30. (*National Trust*)

The nutshells are a useful reminder of other sorts of foodstuffs available from the countryside around the villa. It is a pity we have no pips to show us what sorts of fruit were being eaten at the villa, and most probably grown not far from it. Several of the species with which we are familiar, such as cherry and medlar, seem to have been introduced to Britain in the Roman period, as well as new vegetables such as cucumber; the latter reminds us that we know very little about which vegetables available in Roman Britain, including peas and beans as well as the cabbage family, were eaten here, and little about vegetable types such as lentils and other pulses. The Roman period saw the introduction of a range of herbs and spices as well, presumably a reflection of the adoption of Mediterranean cooking styles.

A quantity of animal bone was recovered from the layers of soil dumped to level up the garden court, which was presumably rubbish from elsewhere in the villa. The principal animals represented were the standard trio of cattle, sheep/goat and pig: the main domesticated livestock of the Roman period. Pig has historically been kept essentially as a food animal; indeed, its carcass yields little else of use to humans save the skin. Cattle and sheep on the other hand are more complex. Certainly both can be raised for their meat, preferably killed when young but this is not essential, and the fact that the bones under consideration here bore cut marks from knives or cleavers and were very fragmented strongly suggests butchery for cooking. On the other hand, sheep were a source of wool, probably the principal fibre used in Roman Britain for the manufacture of textiles. It is always important to estimate the age at death of an animal, since if it was kept into maturity this suggests that wool was at least as important, if not more important, than increasingly aged mutton.

Likewise, cattle when alive could be of considerable use: for milk and thus dairy products (some fragments of pottery vessels that could have been used for straining and pressing cheeses have been recovered from the villa); for traction; for manure; or simply as a wealth store (measured by head of cattle). When dead they yielded their skins for leather, as well as bone, sinews and other body parts plus the meat. Even though the waste from the Chedworth garden court does represent the use of these animals as a meat source, they may have had other uses before and after death. In addition, the garden court levelling deposits yielded some bones of domesticated birds in the form of chickens and geese, as well as of game animals, red deer and roe deer as well as the boar mentioned in the last chapter, bringing us back to the role of hunting in the social economy of the villa.

How often meat, domesticated or wild, was eaten is impossible to know from this evidence. Meat cost a lot to produce and would probably rarely have formed part of the meals of the servants and labourers on the estate. On the other hand, varieties of meat in abundance and skilfully and ingeniously prepared would have been an important element in the entertainment of honoured guests, even if the day-to-day diet, even of the *dominus* and his close family, may not have been as extravagant.

The amount of direct evidence is limited, but it does allow us to reconstruct to an extent the sorts of landscapes which supplied the villa, some of them probably close in to it. Obviously the main requirements were for arable land, for the growing of crops along with pasture for cattle and sheep and access to water for these animals, especially for the cattle which required considerable quantities. These animals could, of course, also be turned onto arable fields after harvest to graze as well as to restore soil fertility with their manure. Pigs required less care and maintenance and could be turned out to graze on

44. Part of a pottery cheese press. (*Graham Norrie/University of Birmingham*)

the woodland floor for nutrition such as nuts, pannage, though there would have to be some means of ensuring they did not just disappear.

Woodland was a more important resource than is often recognised. Wood was central to the way of life in the ancient world, and indeed, in all periods down to the very recent past when artificial substitutes, above all plastics, started to be devised. To take the Chedworth villa: wood was necessary for construction, especially of the roofs, possibly also of the floors; for furniture; for transport (wagons and so on); for utensils, especially their handles; for the fuel to heat the hypocausts or braziers that made the villa habitable in winter, to say nothing of firing up the baths that were so central to social life and upper-class grooming. Each of these needs required different types of timber, since different types have different characteristics, of different scantling (dimensions) and thus of different ages. Woodland management would have to be undertaken over the long term to ensure the availability of certain types of slow-growing timber such as oak. Shorter-term measures, such as coppicing, would provide the smaller woods for such things as handles for tools or fuel for the baths.

Woodland could also have been used for raising game for hunting, such as the red and roe deer for which we have evidence from the site.

Thus the evidence of grain and animal bones from the villa does allow us to envisage the countryside around it in a general way. It allows us to consider some of the types of agricultural labourer that would have been needed: the ploughmen, the cowherds, shepherds and swineherds, possibly a miller; and some of the animals that might have been needed for labour, such as oxen for the plough teams and probably also for traction for carts, and horses, especially for the *dominus* and his family, and possibly donkeys, both for riding and for turning the mill if it was not powered by the Coln. These in turn suggest there would have to be grooms, stable boys, possibly a blacksmith or farrier for all the ironworking needed for such an establishment. All these people, and possibly their wives and children, could then be called upon for labour-intensive parts of the agricultural year such as the harvest.

THE VILLA & THE WIDER ECONOMY

Some of this produce would remain within the estate, supplying the villa and its inhabitants and possibly also in part the estate workers and their families. The surpluses over and above this would need to be converted into things that were useful to the *dominus* and the estate; otherwise there would be little point in producing them at all. This is where the estate had to interact with the wider economy, at local, provincial, inter-provincial and imperial levels. First, we shall look at the imperial level, since it was one of the most important conditioning factors for the economy of the empire as a whole, and because it ultimately lay behind the presence at the villa of one of the most recognisable of all imperial Roman objects: coins.

The imperial system, set in place by the first Emperor Augustus (31 BC–AD 14), was a thinly veiled military dictatorship, with the armies securing the physical safety of the emperor (or on occasion not), defending the borderlands of the empire against attack, providing internal security, and at times expanding the *imperium* (rule) of the Roman People: on this rested all the other attributes of imperial power and administration. This meant that the emperor had inescapable financial obligations: chiefly the payment and supply of the armies, but also administration, imperial projects, largesse and benefits to individuals and communities. Where there are central state obligations, there are taxes to pay for them. In the ancient world the two things that were

45. A *denarius* of Lucilla, sister of the Emperor Commodus (180–192) from Chedworth villa. (Scale 1cm). (*Graham Norrie/University of Birmingham*)

most common and most easily taxed were land and people; by the fourth century these were the subject of the *iugatio* (property tax) and *capitatio* (poll tax) respectively. In order for these to be assessed and collected there needed to be censuses of land and people, assessments of their tax obligations and a mechanism for extracting the tax. For the censuses and assessments there was the department of the imperial finance minister, the grandly titled *Comes Sacrarum Largitionum* (Count of the Sacred Largesses); despite his title, he was as much if not more concerned with getting money than with doling it out (late Roman officialdom was master of the branch of linguistic dishonesty that we now call management-speak).

Collecting the tax assessments was one of the duties of the local land-owning class who formed the councils of the cities and their territories. They regarded this as burdensome since they were personally responsible for any shortfall; their efforts to make sure there was no shortfall (possibly even some profit) meant their inferiors hated the system. The whole thing contrived to be rampantly corrupt and wildly inefficient. Repeated imperial edicts attempting to enforce the proper collection of tax show that the system did not work properly; the fact that the emperors had to repeat these edicts shows that their sacred majesties had a lot less effective power than we might suppose. Tax could be rendered either in kind, such as grain, animals or other supplies that went direct to the consumer (the army), or in gold or silver (coins or other objects) to pay the army and discharge other imperial obligations.

COINS

The owner of a villa such as Chedworth, therefore, would have had tax obligations. In addition, he would want to dispose of his surplus produce and obtain
goods and services not provided for on the estate; in late Roman Britain this
could in part be done through the use of money. These factors ultimately lie
behind the presence at the Chedworth villa of some 400 Roman coins, a
class of object that can tell us a good deal about the villa in the wider Roman
world. Coin was struck by the Roman authorities as a means of paying the
army and others; it was not supplied primarily to lubricate the wheels of
commerce as it is now. In the closing decades BC Augustus had reformed the
existing coinage to provide for denominations in gold (the *aureus*), silver (the
denarius) and various forms of copper alloy (*sestertius*, *as*), all in precise relationships to each other. This system worked tolerably well for two centuries, but
the third century saw major changes and a crisis in the coinage, in the depths
of which gold was hardly struck, silver was massively debased, becoming in
effect a bronze coin with a silver wash, and the old bronze denominations
almost disappeared.

At the turn of the third and fourth centuries the system was stabilised and
a tri-metallic coinage re-established in gold (the *solidus*), silver (the *miliarensis*)
and various copper-alloy denominations (the *nummus* and others). Therefore,
in the fourth century, someone like the owner of Chedworth had to turn
surplus into gold and silver either by purchase in exchange for produce, or
by going to a money-changer (*nummularius*). A *nummularius* would have had
access through the authorities to large quantities of low-value copper-alloy
coin, which the state minted essentially to buy in the gold and silver that were
its main concern. If the public wished to use coins for buying and selling, the
state knew perfectly well that this was another function of its production of
coin. The presence of coins at the Chedworth villa shows on the one hand
that the inhabitants were tied into the state's fiscal cycles by the obligation to
pay tax, and on the other hand that coins tied them into wider commerce
through their use for buying and selling.

Which coins have been recorded from the Chedworth villa? We can be sure
that the 1864 excavations will not have recovered all the coins present, since
clearance with pick and shovel is not a method of excavation well adapted to
finding coins. Nevertheless, some were found, as Farrer noted in 1865, and
subsequent excavations on the villa to modern standards have led to many
more being found and recorded. Currently, there are just under 400 coins
known from the villa, minted under emperors from the middle of the first

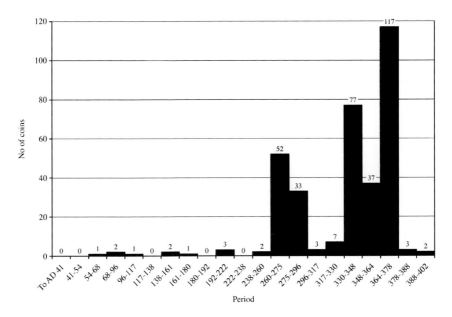

46. A histogram of coins from Chedworth. (*Henry Buglass/University of Birmingham*)

century (Nero) to the turn of the fourth and fifth centuries (Arcadius). The graph shows the distribution of their minting dates (the periods given are the ones conventionally used by numismatists to separate out Roman coins into chronological blocks). It clearly divides into two parts: the mid-first century to the mid-third century, where there are very few coins; and the later third century to the turn of the fourth and fifth centuries, where the majority of the coins lie, with some periods showing major peaks.

How should we interpret this pattern? The first thing to say is that it is a variant of the pattern found on almost all Romano-British sites that, like Chedworth, were occupied for most of the Roman period; Chedworth's pattern is not, therefore, peculiar. It is necessary to look at the contrasting nature of coins before and after 260, in particular the copper-alloy issues. No gold and few silver coins have been found at Chedworth: they were too intrinsically valuable and if dropped would be looked for. The same in many ways was true of the copper-alloy issues of the first and second centuries: they were of some value and moreover were large and quite heavy (more like a 50p than a 5p), so more noticeable if dropped and worth the effort to recover. Also, they seem not to have been supplied in large quantities to Britain from the mint at Rome, increasing their rarity. They were probably used for relatively costly purchases, cheaper things being bartered. The first half of the third century

47. A *denarius* of the Emperor Caracalla (211–218) from Chedworth. (*Graham Norrie/University of Birmingham*)

saw very few coins being supplied to Britain; this accounts for the penury of coins at Chedworth during the first 200 years of Roman rule in Britain: there probably were never many coins at the site and on the whole they were too valuable to lose.

However, the 260s and 270s saw the final debasement of the once silver denominations to less than 5 per cent silver; they had effectively become bronze coins. They were struck and supplied in great quantities, presumably because it had proved impossible to sustain a high face value for them so many more were needed. An unintended consequence of this seems to have been that the provincial populations got used to relatively abundant, low-value coinage, of low enough value for day-to-day buying and selling. In the last quarter of the third century the state was making efforts to reform the coinage and increase its value and purchasing power, and this meant again that relatively few of these new, larger, higher-value coins got into circulation.

It seems that many in the provincial populations had come rather to like the convenience of an abundant, low-value coinage, so to counter the shortage of the official issues, they produced their own counterfeit coinages: illegal but the state had no police or other force to stop them. What people did, naturally enough, was to copy the imperial issues which they had got used to handling. In the third century one of the most distinctive features of the coinage was the emperor's head, shown wearing a crown representing the sun's rays – a 'radiate' crown; the imitations from the late third century always show this feature. Yet from being reasonably close to the official originals in

48. A 'radiate' coin of the Emperor Valerian (253–260) from Chedworth. (*Graham Norrie/ University of Birmingham*)

size, weight and workmanship, they rapidly declined into small, mis-struck scraps of bronze – 'barbarous radiates'. Comparing them with official issues one wonders how the copies could have possibly been regarded as anything like the real thing; but if people accepted them, perhaps even in only limited areas, then that was enough. It is these coins that account for the first two periods at Chedworth showing major peaks: Period 13 (260–275) and Period 14 (275–296), where the majority of the coins are 'barbarous radiates'.

'Barbarous radiates' probably continued to be struck and to circulate into the opening decades of the fourth century, but by the 320s the reformed bronze coinage of the state had declined in size and weight back to a low standard, so these issues, which were struck in large quantities, displaced the 'barbarous radiates'. The process that had brought the 'barbarous radiates' into being continued to operate through the fourth century. Sometimes the state struck and supplied to Britain large quantities of low-value bronze; at other times there were long periods (over a decade sometimes) when it did not. These periods of low or no supply saw the production of counterfeits using the newest official issues as models; in this way the circulating pool of low-value coinage was maintained. This accounts for the peaks in Period 17 (330–348) and Period 18 (348–364), the latter part of the reign of Constantine I (306–337) and the reigns of his sons (the House of Constantine) in the 340s and 350s. Again, most of the coins of these periods found at Chedworth were copies.

Yet why were so many of these coins found? It is quite plausible that rather than being 'lost', the usual shorthand used by numismatists, they were actually

49. A coin of the Emperor Constantine I (306–337). (*Graham Norrie/University of Birmingham*)

discarded as new, abundant imperial issues came in: people were literally throwing away money, probably because it had become worthless. This could be what happened in the 360s and 370s as the last great imperial issue flooded in to Britain: the coins of the brother emperors, in the West Valentinian I (364–375) and in the East Valens (364–378), Period 19, driving out the inferior copies of the House of Constantine of the 350s. The next two periods, 20 and 21 (378–388, 388–402), saw the last imperial coins to be supplied to Britain, in low numbers. Interestingly, these decades of low supply did not provoke another major outbreak of counterfeiting; perhaps the massive issues of Period 19 tided the coinage over, or perhaps the demand for low-value coin was dropping.

It is clear that the pattern of coins from Chedworth says little or nothing about the history of the villa. It does not mean that there were more people living there in the later Roman period than the earlier (though there probably were) or that for some reason people were more adept at losing coins. Instead, it says a great deal about the value, weight and supply of the coinage and the uses to which it was put. In the later third and fourth centuries many people in Roman Britain seem to have become used to using low-value coins; this is particularly evident at towns and in the countryside, at sites such as villas which were tied into the wider economy. Simpler rural sites tend to produce far fewer coins, suggesting their inhabitants' contact with the coin-using part of the economy was more sporadic. As argued earlier, the presence of these coins from late Roman Chedworth must in part be to do with the need to meet tax obligations (however unwillingly); it must also be to do with the use of coinage in a commercial context for buying and selling. This put Chedworth in contact with the commercial currents throughout Britain and in the western provinces of the empire more widely, and we have one type of find that gives us some perception of those currents: pottery.

POTTERY

The great majority of the pottery found at Chedworth in the 1864 excavations and, it has to be admitted, in those of the 1950s and '60s was thrown away, with only a few of the more complete or more decorative pieces being retained. These are essentially useless for our purposes, since we need to be able to quantify all the pottery from the villa, the ordinary as well as the unusual, in order to get a truer picture of the areas from which the villa was deriving its supplies and how frequently it was in contact with these areas. Therefore, we are dependent on the figures and analyses of the pottery from recent excavations for a more comprehensive picture, except these excavations produced much less pottery than the 1864 excavations would have, had all their pottery been kept. Study of the pottery from these recent excavations, and comparisons with evidence from other excavations on Roman sites in the Cotswolds, demonstrates that the earliest pottery was of types introduced in the second half of the second century. Internationally, these included small quantities of amphorae from southern Spain; these were large, globular ceramic containers for olive oil, of a type produced in massive quantities in the first and second centuries in the valley of the river the Romans called the Baetis, now the Guadalquivir. Most of these amphorae probably arrived in Britain as part of the supply chain bringing Mediterranean products and comforts to the army, but it is interesting that the desire for olive oil had spread to the civilian market also; whether this was for Roman-style cooking, anointing in Roman-style bathing, or fuelling Roman-style lamps we cannot tell for Chedworth. Other amphora fragments attest to the importation of Gaulish wine.

Also from Gaul came what British archaeologists call samian, the red-gloss pottery, sometimes with relief decoration, manufactured in great centres in central Gaul in the second century and in eastern Gaul (west of the Rhine) on into the early third century. Despite being inherently fragile, this pottery was transported hundreds of miles, again partly to meet military demand but

50. A sherd of an amphora from Chedworth. (*Graham Norrie/University of Birmingham*)

increasingly to meet civilian demand as fine tableware. Other good-quality pottery of this date at Chedworth was fine drinking vessels with a high-gloss black coating from factories in central Gaul and around Cologne. However, distinctive and interesting as these wares are, they comprised only a tiny proportion of the pottery of this date from the site; the overwhelming majority was produced in the region, probably in the upper Thames valley, the Severn valley and north Wiltshire particularly, and consisted essentially of vessels for storing, preparing, cooking and serving foodstuffs: what archaeologists refer to as 'coarse wares'. It was cheap and serviceable earthenware, sometimes with a colour wash or simple, patterned surface decoration.

By the fourth century, the patterns of pottery found at the villa had changed markedly. No more were amphorae of olive oil being imported from Spain and the samian industries of Gaul had ceased mass production and export in the first part of the third century. Instead, the pottery was of British manufacture. The disappearance of the olive oil trade was partly to do with the decline of this industry in its south Spanish homeland, possibly because provincial tastes had changed and olive oil was no longer so desirable. The decline in samian imports may have in part been hidden by the rise of British centres which produced glossy red pottery in the samian tradition.

The largest of these was on the middle Thames in modern Oxfordshire, centring on the area of what is now Oxford. Its products are present in some quantities at Chedworth, presumably shipped up the Thames to near Cirencester, as well as transported by road, with smaller quantities of similar so-called 'fine wares' from centres in the New Forest and the Nene valley around modern Peterborough.

From the second century through to the third and fourth centuries there was one workaday type of pottery that came from further afield: this was the 'Black Burnished ware' produced round Poole Harbour. Technologically, it was very simple, being largely made by hand rather than on the potter's wheel. From the early second century it had achieved a wide distribution in Britain, including up to the northern frontiers, and by the fourth century it was also common across the Channel in north-western Gaul. Why this simple, largely undecorated pottery which was comparable with many

51. A *mortarium* (grinding/mixing bowl) found at Chedworth. (*Graham Norrie/University of Birmingham*)

other types of workaday pottery produced in Roman Britain achieved such wide distribution remains a mystery. Nevertheless, it is present in quantity at Chedworth from the second century on. Of course, neither Black Burnished ware nor the other simpler types of pottery would have appeared on the table of the *dominus* and his family; they would have been served either on metals such as pewter or possibly bronze, silver at the most lavish banquets, with perhaps the more carefully produced types of Oxford ware for less formal dining. This is something that has to be remembered when we study pottery from the Roman or other periods; it is important to archaeologists because it survives. To people at the time it was probably far less important than a range of other things such as foodstuffs, textiles, woodwork, that were much more common but rarely survive today. Therefore, pottery has to act as a proxy for these other materials.

So what do the origins and circulation of pottery tell us about the wider contacts of the Chedworth villa and its relation to the commercial life of the region in the fourth century?

CONTACTS & COMMERCE

It is highly unlikely that anything other than a small proportion of the manufactured goods used at Chedworth villa were traded directly to the villa because they were made locally or because they were brought in by the Roman equivalents of chapmen or pedlars. It may be that the source of some of the coarse wares of which we do not know the manufacturing site will turn out to be very local to the villa; they may even have been produced on its estates and thus formed part of the supply of foodstuffs, services and goods directly to the big house. However, Oxford wares, for instance, were so widely distributed across southern Britain that it would have been hugely inefficient to try to merchandise them by selling directly in penny quantities from producer to consumer; they must have been made available in much larger quantities through some sort of market system.

Where would the inhabitants of Chedworth turn for manufactured goods, for foodstuffs they did not produce themselves, for luxury goods and for specialist services such as law or education? The obvious answer lay some 8 Roman miles away as the *corvus* flew: Cirencester (see colour plate 26).

Cirencester, *Corinium*, had developed as the chief administrative centre, market and conurbation of the Roman local government district created out of the pre-Conquest people the Romans called the Dobunni, who probably occupied much of the Cotswolds and west across the Severn valley. The area around Cirencester was important before the Roman invasion, and soon after the invasion a garrison fort was set up in the valley of the River Churn on what was to become the centre of the Roman city. When in due course the army moved out, the site was constituted as a city and administrative centre and over time the landed wealthy of the area had a grid of streets laid out and they adorned their city with public buildings and monuments, such as a forum for administration and law, baths for grooming the Roman body, an amphitheatre for ritualised violence and possibly a theatre for dramatic productions, and eventually large residences for them to inhabit, either all the time or when they came in from their country estates. By the early fourth century, Cirencester had been encircled with the second longest set of defences in Britain after London, consisting of a second-century earth rampart later fronted by a stone wall, enclosing an area of 97 hectares (240 acres).

By the fourth century, Cirencester may also have been promoted to the rank of provincial capital. The Emperor Diocletian (284–305) subdivided many existing provinces into smaller ones, probably to make them easier to administer. The original single province of Britain had been divided into two at the start of the third century, and was now further subdivided to produce a total of four British provinces. One of the very few late Roman inscriptions from Britain comes from Cirencester and refers to the restoration of a column to the traditional religions (see also p. 101) by the governor of one of the four British provinces, *Britannia Prima*. This only shows that Cirencester was in *Britannia Prima*, not necessarily that it was its capital; but given that Cirencester was by that time the largest city in south-western Britain by far, it is not unlikely that it was the provincial capital. Some of the public buildings and monuments constructed in the first and second centuries were probably still in use and there were now a number of the richer residences we call 'town-houses'. As such, the city must have served as a major economic centre, servicing its considerable resident population, including the governor and his entourage, and offering raw materials, manufactured goods, luxury goods (for instance, mosaics) and specialist services such as law or education to its catchment area, within which lay the Chedworth villa. Trade in the lower-value goods and services would undoubtedly have been helped by the existence of the plentiful, low-denomination coinage (and copies) of the later third and fourth centuries.

Chedworth had good communications with Cirencester. Not far to the east lay one of the major arterial roads of Roman Britain, running from the

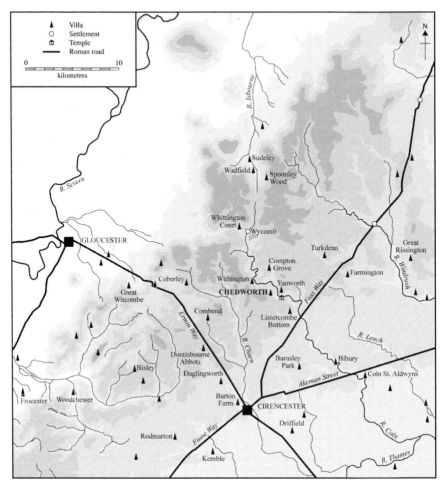

52. Map of the roads and villas in the Chedworth area. (*Henry Buglass/University of Birmingham*)

Exeter area up through Cirencester and on to Lincoln: what we call the Fosse Way. It is an example of what we term a 'Roman road', a long-distance road laid out in long, straight stretches and built up on an artificial base, an *agger*, and metalled with crushed stone or gravel. It is important to realise that such roads were a tiny minority of all the thousands of miles of roads and tracks criss-crossing Roman Britain. The maps showing only these 'Roman roads' are rather like a modern road map showing only motorways and dual carriageways. The Fosse Way crossed the Coln valley some 4 miles east of the Chedworth villa at modern Fossebridge. From there it would have been an easy walk, ride or cart journey on a lesser road along the floor of the valley, passing the temple and thus arriving at the villa.

The villa also lay close to one of the few roads we know of in Roman Britain that, although not a long-distance route like the Fosse Way, was nevertheless laid out in straight sections and metalled: this was what is now called the White Way. Leaving Cirencester by the same gate as the Fosse Way, it struck northwards along the crest on the eastern side of the valley of the River Churn. It then bent north-north-eastwards to bring it to the southern edge of the Coln valley a little over 1km (just under 1 mile) west of the villa, before descending the side of the valley to cross the river, probably somewhere in the vicinity of present-day Cassey Compton. Where it went after that, if indeed it did continue, we do not know. The Chedworth villa would have been very well sited to take advantage of this shorter route into Cirencester, one which was convenient not only for those on foot or on horse, but also for carts transporting bulk produce into the provincial capital. Such ability to dispose of surplus goods in return for a whole range of merchandise and services was one of the hallmarks of the Roman period in Britain.

THE COTSWOLD VILLAS

Cirencester lay at the heart of one of the most important concentrations of villas in Roman Britain, which by the fourth century was notable for the number of villas, their decoration such as mosaics, and in some cases their great size and lavish appointments. Chedworth's place in this social and cultural landscape needs some consideration, along with why such groupings came into being both in Britain and more widely within the western Roman Empire at this date.

To start at the local level, the Coln valley upstream of where the river was crossed by the Fosse Way had a string of villas. Between the crossing and Chedworth villa there is the site at Listercombe Bottom in a small re-entrant valley opening off the western side of the river valley, similar to the setting of the Chedworth villa. Trenched at various occasions, it had a bathhouse (yielding tiles stamped ARVERI, see p. 172), possibly a mosaic and traces of a number of buildings. Across the Coln from the Chedworth villa, there was a Romano-British site in Yanworth Wood. Too little is known of it to be sure whether it was another villa or something less substantial. A villa lay at Compton Grove, south-west of the present village of Compton Abdale. Like the Chedworth villa it sat in a small, east-facing re-entrant valley which opened on to the larger valley of a stream running north–south to join the Coln.

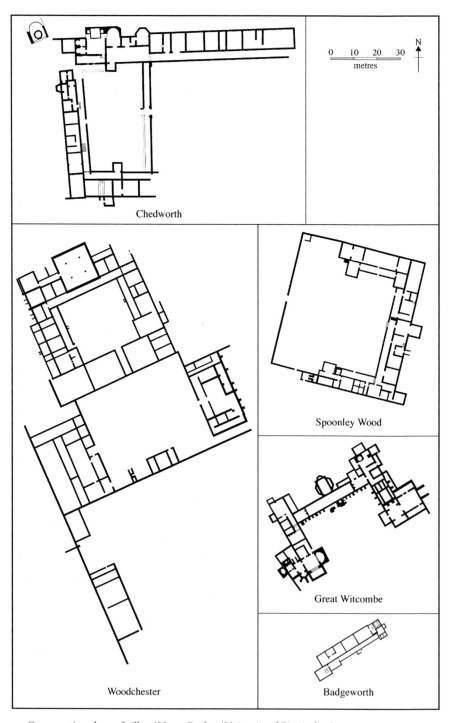

53. Comparative plans of villas. (*Henry Buglass/University of Birmingham*)

Upstream of this, in the modern parish of Withington, lay two sites, each of which can qualify as a villa. One of these sites, excavated in 1811, consisted of a so-called 'aisled barn' or aisled building, a rectangular structure with two rows of internal posts supporting the roof; later, the interior was divided up into a number of rooms, many with mosaic floors, and a small bathhouse was added. More recently, another site was discovered beside the Coln and not far from a spring called Wall Well; a *Time Team* excavation encountered part of a bathhouse with a mosaic of fourth-century date. Further still up the Coln, nearer its source at Syreford, was a rather different type of Roman settlement, at Wycomb in the parish of Andoversford. Rather than being the relatively small (usually under 3ha or 7 acres), tightly organised site characteristic of a villa, this was a sprawling site covering some 11ha (27 acres) and consisting of a number of separate structures, including a temple, organised along a road with side streets branching off it. It is difficult to be sure of its precise functions, but it may have acted as a local market and religious focus for the people at the top end of the Coln valley and the surrounding area.

The string of villas along the middle Coln valley, of which Chedworth was one, seem to have shared certain characteristics. The first is that they all lay within the river valley rather than on the higher, rolling tablelands of the Cotswolds. This might in part have been because these situations were more sheltered. It might also have been because access to the river was important, although Chedworth, Compton Grove, Listercombe and the recent site at Withington either certainly or probably had their own water source as well; the river was also important for watering livestock and for the well-watered soils of the valley floor. Chedworth, Compton Grove and Listercombe all lay in small, re-entrant valleys facing east, looking out over the main valley or, in the case of Compton Grove, the valley of a tributary stream. This preference for a site in the river valley is noticeable with the next river to the east, the Windrush, and its tributaries such as the Sherborne Brook, including the massive, recently discovered villa at Turkdean, also the focus of a *Time Team* excavation. To the west, the Churn has fewer known villas, though there are examples at The Ditches, Bagendon and Combe End, Colesbourne.

The term 'villa' is a very elastic one; since it essentially refers to a rural structure with a building or buildings in the 'Roman style', the term encompasses everything from a simple farmhouse to something on the scale of a grand country house. We therefore need to compare the Chedworth villa with others from the region in order to gauge its place in the social hierarchy. The Cotswold villa plans reproduced demonstrate this range; the smallest ones exemplified by Badgeworth are simple dwellings of a few rooms, in this case fronted by a 'winged-corridor facade' of a gallery along the front of the building flanked by two projecting rooms. When compared with sites such as Great Witcombe, Spoonley Wood in Sudeley or indeed the Chedworth villa itself, these simple villas are clearly not in the same league. What distinguishes the three sites just mentioned is first of all that the 'footprint' of the buildings is much larger: there are many more rooms, some clearly important reception rooms; there is a sense of architectural coherence and elaboration; the principal residential areas are physically separated from more workaday areas; and excavation has yielded mosaics and other signs of elaborate decoration. Such villas were more than simply agricultural centres; they were places where the owners could represent themselves as persons of wealth, influence and taste in order to overawe their subordinates, compete with their peers and try to impress their superiors.

Up a step in size and elaboration was the recently discovered complex at Turkdean, which seems to have been arranged around three courtyards. The most impressive of all was the massive complex at Woodchester, near modern-day Stroud, which boasted three axial courtyards of progressively decreasing size, presumably reflecting diminishing accessibility by social status, arriving finally at the principal reception room with its enormous Orpheus mosaic, other mosaic-floored galleries and chambers around the inner court, one of which seems to have been a sculpture gallery with imported marble pieces. This villa was of a size and magnificence to rival others in the Mediterranean heartlands of the empire. Chedworth clearly approximates more to Woodchester than to Farmington: it does not match the sheer size or the architectural and decorative elaboration of Woodchester, yet with its reception rooms, bath suites, mosaics and sculptures it is clearly from the same social and cultural context. The difference between the Chedworth and Woodchester villas is one of degree, not of type, and one could well imagine the social gradations between the *domini* of the two establishments and the consequent opportunities for the sorts of competitive display touched on in previous chapters. The same would go for other villas such as Spoonley Wood, where the gap in social status with Chedworth, judging by size and elaboration, seems to have been much less and the opportunities for sharp social competition correspondingly greater.

Can we plot the distribution of villas of this larger sort and seek to understand why they are where they are (and are not)? Fortunately, we now have a catalogue of all the mosaics known from Roman Britain, and as we have seen, mosaics were an essential element of status display, so their distribution, especially where they occur in quantity, can be taken as an index of where the

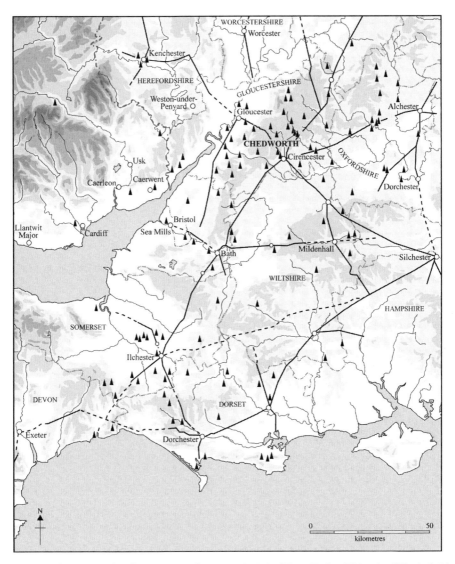

54. Map of mosaics in fourth-century south-western Britain. (*Henry Buglass/University of Birmingham*)

more elaborate villas were. The distribution map of fourth-century mosaics in south-western Britain shows clearly that they were not evenly distributed across this part of Roman Britain: on the one hand, they clustered in the band near the Fosse Way around the Roman centres at Dorchester, Ilchester and Cirencester; on the other hand, they were almost absent from what is now Wales and extremely rare in the counties of the Welsh Marches. Just as striking is the way the grouping around Cirencester ends abruptly to the north:

the south-eastern half of modern Warwickshire is essentially a continuation of the Cotswolds, yet the county contains but one certain and one probable site with mosaics. What is the reason for these marked variations?

It might be argued that the sites with mosaics in south-western Britain were found mainly along the Jurassic limestones stretching from Somerset through Gloucestershire and Oxfordshire and on through Northamptonshire and into Lincolnshire. In addition, the chalks of Dorset, Hampshire and to an extent Kent show an above-average concentration of mosaics. The argument from geology would be that the limestones supported soils whose properties and drainage were favourable to the raising of the crops and livestock characteristic of the fourth century, and thus these were the areas of Roman Britain that were the wealthiest and could afford the sort of expenditure involved in commissioning mosaics. However, there is a two-fold problem for this. One is that the correspondence between these areas supposedly favourable to such wealth accumulations and the incidence of mosaics is not an exact fit. We noted above the lack of mosaics in modern south-eastern Warwickshire, which in terms of geology and soils is not unlike the Cotswolds. On a larger scale, while some of the chalk lands of southern Britain have a relatively dense distribution of mosaics, others, for instance in East Anglia, do not; yet the finds of fourth-century silver plate and jewellery from this region show that there was significant wealth there.

The other problem is that there are areas that are rich agriculturally but which do not opt for the villa as the means to express that wealth. We have just noted the case of East Anglia, long a highly productive and wealthy region. Closer to Chedworth and the Cotswolds there are counties such as Herefordshire, Worcestershire and Shropshire, again very productive agriculturally but yielding minute numbers of mosaics. Therefore, simple geological determinism will not suffice; there must be other reasons.

The almost total absence of mosaics from Wales and their rarity in the neighbouring counties is part of a wider pattern that helps us understand these questions. In what are now Devon and Cornwall, Wales and England north and west of a line from the Severn to the Humber, there are very few mosaics compared with the regions to their south and east. And not just mosaics: towns, villas, temples, burials and many other markers of the impact of Roman culture on Britain lie overwhelmingly in the south and east. In the north and west it appears they simply did not matter to the people there; other things must have. Though people in the north and west might have had the means to invest in villas and mosaics, they did not; it was a matter of cultural framework, practice and choice. In some regions and areas the social and cultural expectation was that surplus wealth was to be expended in the sorts of status display that we see materialised at Chedworth and in the Cotswolds more generally, invested in solid and immobile display such as masonry villas; but in East Anglia, for instance, portable displays of wealth, such as silver plate, seem to have been more the norm (there are villas there also, but not the quantity or elaboration of the Cotswolds ones). The question then arises of why Chedworth and the Cotswolds made the choices they did.

The masonry villa, mosaics, sculpture and the sorts of activities these seem to be associated with, such as receiving guests, hunting, dining, and being the educated host, hark back to the traditional view of how a Roman aristocrat should spend his days when engaged in *otium*, i.e. useful and productive leisure on his country estates. It is thus making a statement about how the *dominus* wished to see himself and to be seen, in a traditional Roman social and cultural framework. Other leaders of society in late Roman Britain chose to represent their status in different ways. This presumably, in part, explains the regional nature of such means of display. The landowning classes of a region would be competitive with each other; they would therefore wish to use a common vocabulary for competition so that different degrees of wealth, education and taste could be measured against a commonly accepted scale. In the Cotswolds the means of competition had chosen this traditionalist frame of reference, though of course it would be tradition reinterpreted and reinvented: a fourth-century banquet would not have been the same as a second-century one.

It is also clear that this competition had a chronological dimension as well as a geographical one. Chedworth is a good example of this: its origins in the second century were much more modest than its grandiose fourth-century form. The same is true of other major, fourth-century Cotswold villas such as Great Witcombe, Spoonley or Woodchester; they all developed from simpler beginnings. So in the Cotswold region in the fourth century there were powerful social and cultural forces propelling landowners to display their wealth and status in this particular way. Equally, there were other, neighbouring regions operating within an alternative framework of values and expectations where the means of expressing wealth and status were very different. What these other means were is often very difficult to detect in the archaeology, for instance in regions such as Wales or the Marches. Nor do we as yet understand why there can be sharp breaks between one regional tradition and another, as, for instance, at the north end of the Cotswold villa tradition. Does this correspond to a political boundary, for example between the Dobunni and the administrative area to their north (the Cornovii)? Since the administrative unit of the Dobunni seems to have included areas west of the Severn, with few if any villas and mosaics, this would seem not to be the whole answer. As yet we cannot answer the question. This is partly because the tradition of the study of Roman Britain and of the Roman impact on Britain has placed a premium on sites and regions where that Roman impact is visible, through such things as villas and mosaics, and these have become the index against which to measure the success or failure of an area in its response to Roman values. It is only recently that archaeologists have appreciated that there could have been other ways for people to make distinctions between themselves, ones that do not measure up so well against our modern scale of values, but which mattered at the time.

There is one further feature of the Cotswold group, and other similar groups in Britain, that might give us part of an answer as to why these areas adopted this particular vocabulary of display (though it is of limited help in understanding areas that did not). Regions where there was a marked preference for lavish villas as a means of social and cultural exhibition were in fact not that common across the western empire in the fourth century. The main ones were: south-western Gaul (roughly modern-day Aquitaine); the Mediterranean coastline of Spain; the north-central area of Spain (the northern *meseta*); southern Portugal; and the area around Trier on the Moselle. This is not to say there were no villas elsewhere, but they were few by comparison with these regions. There is a pattern of clusters and (relative) absences rather than a more uniform distribution. The regions of Britain where villas were important in the fourth century, therefore, fit into a wider pattern and if we can understand what factors were conditioning the wider pattern we might have a better understanding of the driving forces in Britain.

It is perhaps the cluster around Trier that gives a way in. For much of the fourth century, Trier was the residence of the emperor or other member of the imperial family; even when it was not, it was far and away the most important administrative centre west of the Alps. The huge complex of buildings of this imperial residence is only partially known, but it is in an architectural and decorative language of reception rooms, baths, courtyards and colonnades, mosaics and marble. It is in many ways a rich villa writ very large and it served as a model for how aristocrats should express their wealth and power through their residences. Ambitious men would tend to gravitate towards Trier to seek preferment, and having experienced the imperial palace this would be the language of power that they would have become familiar with and might then use in their homelands showing their links with the greatest power in the empire. The effects of this can be seen around Trier itself in the fourth-century villas and residences of the region, some of them almost certainly in imperial ownership. Can this argument be extended to the other great clusters of villas in the fourth-century West?

The evidence is fragmentary but may point in this direction. For instance, Ausonius, a *grammaticus* of Bordeaux (see p. 79), was summoned to Trier to act as tutor to Gratian, son of the western Emperor Valentinian I. He subsequently rose high in the imperial service, with his family in tow. Some of his forebears had also been in the imperial service. If his family was at all representative of the Aquitanian nobility, then the region's aristocracy might well have been familiar with and indebted to the imperial vocabulary of power and wealth. Likewise, the central northern area of Spain seems to have been where the family of Theodosius I 'the Great', in the late fourth century the last ruler of an undivided and undiminished Roman Empire, was based, and there is other evidence for involvement with the imperial court from the region. If this argument is along the right lines, one can see why these regional aristocracies might have wished to deploy the traditional language of the old senatorial nobility and the imperial court to make their position clear. Other aristocracies elsewhere in the west took different decisions; for instance, the aristocracies of northern Gaul seem to have relied much more on the vocabulary of military power and rank as a way of proclaiming their position, and villas were few and far between and not very lavish. If this argument has merit, then the consequences for the villa-rich areas of fourth-century Britain would seem to be that they too contained aristocrats who were implicated in the imperial service and wished to deploy that vocabulary to state their rank and links with the central authorities of the empire. If so, then this has interesting repercussions for how we should view an aristocracy that we have traditionally studied in an insular way, seeing them in their British context only rather than taking account of their possible wider connections.

This chapter has taken us a long way in trying to understand the Chedworth villa, from considering its immediate physical environs to speculating upon its wider connections and significance at the level of the western Roman Empire and its rulers. This is in its way entirely logical. Everyone operates in different circles, larger and smaller, and all of us make different statements about ourselves to different audiences. The Roman period in Britain meant that the inhabitants, especially those with the means to be in contact with wider trends, had a whole new set of audiences to address and a new set of ways of addressing them. In the preceding chapters we have often drawn upon evidence from Britain more widely and from outside Britain to suggest why the physical remains of the Chedworth villa are the way they are, and what this tells us about the social structures, the lives and cultural framework of the people at the villa, especially the *dominus* and his immediate family. Though our focus of study has been on one villa in one place at one time, the study is only possible if we place that villa and its people in the wider setting of the Roman Empire in the fourth century, the heyday of the Chedworth villa.

SEVEN

OBLIVION AND REDISCOVERY

How did such an impressive complex of buildings fall into ruin, to be covered by earth and vegetation; what happened to them over the long stretch of time between the fifth and the nineteenth centuries; and how were they rediscovered, uncovered and put on view? These are the questions that will occupy this chapter, to bring the story of the Chedworth site from its late Roman heyday up to the present day.

CHEDWORTH & THE END OF ROMAN BRITAIN

The preceding chapters have discussed the Chedworth villa essentially in its most developed form, around the middle of the fourth century. This is a period often seen as the 'golden age' of Roman Britain, the time at which there is most evidence for peace and prosperity, particularly in the many country residences of the period, villas, of which Chedworth is one of the best known. Alternatively, the period can be viewed as an 'Indian summer', a last, late flowering of Roman culture in Britain before the chill winds of the collapse of the western Roman Empire and the loss of the island to Roman rule put an end to this era of plenty for the wealthy. What happened at the end of Roman rule in Britain is best presented in outline first, in order to give a setting against which to place the evidence from Chedworth, which in many ways gives us a microcosm of the wider trends.

The hold of the emperors of Rome remained firm until the end of the fourth century; from 379 until his death in 395, Emperor Theodosius I was the last man to rule the entirety of an undiminished empire. Theodosius was a committed Christian and enactor of legislation against the traditional religions, banning the performance of their rites even in the home. As so often, a strong ruler was succeeded by ineffectual sons. In the West the purple passed to 11-year-old Honorius (d. 423). The first decade of the fifth century was to see events that would ultimately lead to the dissolution of the western empire and the loss of Britain early on in this process.

On the last night of the year 405 a large army of Germanic tribesmen crossed the Roman frontier on the middle Rhine near Mainz. Once across they spread out deep into Gaul, some of them heading south towards the Pyrenees and the Mediterranean. This had important consequences for Britain, although our sources are fragmentary and not at all clear. It seems that the garrison in Britain was fearful that its communications with the Mediterranean heartlands of the empire would be broken and as a consequence, in quick succession, raised three pretenders to the imperial purple. For some unknown reason, the first two of these proved unsatisfactory and were swiftly disposed of; the third, Constantine, proved more durable. A later source tells us he was proclaimed 'on the strength of his name alone'; it was 100 years since the first Christian emperor, Constantine I the Great, had been proclaimed (also illegally) at York. The new Constantine, often called Constantine III, reacted to the crisis by taking troops to Gaul to try to stabilise the military situation there and to prevent the invaders from passing over the Pyrenees into Spain. In both of these he was unsuccessful and in 411 he was eventually brought to bay at Arles in southern Gaul and besieged by forces loyal to Honorius under the general Constantius. Forced to surrender, Constantine was executed while on his way under guard to Honorius at Ravenna in north-eastern Italy.

Honorius and his general Constantius were facing a major military crisis in 411. Not only had the Rhine frontier been badly compromised, with barbarians roaming at will in the interior of Gaul and Spain, but the previous year the Goths, under their king Alaric, had invaded Italy and done the unthinkable: they had captured and sacked Rome. Though the city was no longer the main imperial residence, it was still the largest city in the empire in terms of population and was by far the most important in terms of reputation and past glory; for it to have been sacked was a shock felt throughout the empire.

Faced with a military crisis of this magnitude on the Continent, the recovery of Britain and the restoration of its loyalty to Honorius, though undoubtedly desirable, were impracticable. In fact, the Roman authorities were never able to reimpose their rule on the island and Britain slipped out of the empire.

The consequences of the collapse of Roman rule in Britain are very difficult to assess, because we now enter into the Dark Ages; dark because of the lack of written sources, particularly reliable ones, and dark because the archaeological record drops away to a very low level over much of the fifth century. The troops presumably removed by Constantine III for his campaigning in Gaul were, of course, not sent back or replaced, so the defence of Roman Britain against external enemies was probably much weakened, as would have been internal security. The civilian and financial administrators, who had presumably declared for Constantine III, were also not replaced, so ultimately such aspects as tax would have failed; since much of the tax went to pay the army this may not have been as beneficial as it might sound to modern ears. Such central officials as were left and the local nobilities most likely tried to maintain the Roman system that had been operating on the island for nigh on four centuries and of which they were the chief beneficiaries. However, to judge from the archaeology of this period they were unsuccessful in this.

Forts, towns, villas, temples, all the types of site most intimately connected with and most expressive of Roman power and culture in Britain, seem to have declined rapidly in the first half of the fifth century, and as far as we can tell, by the middle of the century they were almost all abandoned. Any attempt to keep the Roman system running does not seem to have lasted much more than a generation or so. What happened next is very obscure; we are now in the darkest period of the Dark Ages, both historically and archaeologically. Roman Britain probably now fragmented into lots of smaller units ruled over by warlords or chieftains. Rather as in a modern 'collapsed state', the instability and violence of such a situation made a Roman-style way of life impossible, with its need for complex organisation, economic complexity with specialisation of craft and production, and long-distance commerce. Life would have reverted to the local and the short term. Added to this, the few written sources that tell us about Britain at this time are all written from outside Britain and are all insistent on one thing: the island was under attack from the Angles and the Saxons from across the North Sea, from the area that is now northern Holland, north-western Germany and Denmark. These sources believed that by the middle of the fifth century, what had been Roman Britain was rapidly passing under the sway of these peoples, who were eventually to create Angle-land: England.

THE 'DECLINE & FALL' OF THE CHEDWORTH VILLA

How would this developing situation have affected a villa such as Chedworth, and what evidence do we have from the villa itself for what happened there as Roman rule collapsed? Unfortunately, this is a period for which we can say very little because when the villa was uncovered in the 1860s, all the deposits that would have given us some information were shovelled up and thrown away in the search for walls, mosaics and hypocausts. There are only a few scraps of evidence which bear on the problem. These can, however, be supplemented by the results of more recent excavations, particularly in the 1990s on the lower part of the south wing.

There are a number of pieces of evidence, from the parts of the villa exposed in the 1860s, which give an impression of what was happening late in the Roman period. One mosaic, that in Room 28 in the north wing, though relatively large, was of a markedly inferior standard of workmanship when compared with the other large mosaics of the villa; it has been suggested that this means it was of a later date, perhaps towards the end of the fourth century, and there are similar mosaics elsewhere dated to this period. Another mosaic in the north wing, the small one in Room 31a, also seems to have been of poor workmanship. The latest mosaics laid in Roman Britain, in the later fourth century, are generally of poorer quality, from the preparation of the tesserae to the laying out and execution of the design, suggesting there may have been a developing 'skills deficit' in this luxury industry at the time. Staying with the mosaics, in Room 6 a hearth built of tiles was constructed on top of the mosaic in that room, implying that keeping the mosaic in good condition was no longer a priority; times had changed.

Such apparent disrespect for high-quality amenities, in particular mosaics, is a well-known feature of the latest phases of villas in Roman Britain. Building hearths on them was a common practice, as was dividing up rooms by timber partitions set onto or dug into an earlier mosaic; the digging of pits through mosaics was a recurrent feature, as was the dumping of material over mosaics. This used to be called 'squatter occupation', the image being of incoming groups (post-Roman Britons? Anglo-Saxons?) colonising the abandoned residences and caring nothing for the once-grand surroundings. More recent thinking is that these events do not represent the abandonment of a villa followed by the reoccupation by incomers, but rather the final-phase occupation, where the sumptuous lifestyle of the fourth century could no longer be sustained and the priority was of gaining a living by farming, with the former grand apartments turned over either to agricultural uses or to life at a much more basic level of comfort.

55. Looking along the south wing of Chedworth. (*National Trust*)

There are some other pieces of evidence from Chedworth that point in the same direction. A number of the mosaics have traces of burning on their surfaces; this could be evidence for fires or hearths placed directly onto the hard surface provided by the mosaic. The Victorian excavators found a large millstone in Room 30 in the north wing, unlikely to be a relic of the glory days of the villa, but probably evidence for the late use of the buildings. The same excavators also found a large mass of melted lead in Room 27, also in the north wing, which they interpreted as evidence for the villa being destroyed by fire, since they thought the lead was from the roof and had melted and fallen in during the fire. In reality, the Romans rarely used lead for roofing; more likely this represents the recovery of lead from around the villa, from water pipes and bath drains for example, which was melted down for eventual reuse.

In Room 1 the Victorians found a considerable number of coins. Unfortunately they gave no details, but they appear to have been low-value bronze coins. The suggestion was made that Room 1 was the 'steward's room', the room where rent and other fees were paid. If so, the stewards would appear to have had butterfingers. More likely, perhaps, is that the coins were discarded when they no longer had any use, probably somewhere in the first half of the fifth century. Therefore, although the Victorian excavators cleared away the vast bulk of the evidence relating to the final phase of occupation at the villa, enough fragments remain to suggest there was such occupation and that it was very different in character to the fourth-century heyday of the complex.

For more evidence about what happened at the close of the occupation of the villa, we need to turn to the results of the 1997 excavations on part of the lower south wing. As mentioned in Chapter 2, these revealed that there was a wing here at a lower level than the part fronting on to the garden court but reproducing the same basic plan as the rest of the fourth-century villa, namely a gallery with rooms behind. The room exposed in this 8m-wide trench had a channelled hypocaust, though no traces survive of the original floor it supported. This suggests the floor had been deliberately removed. After this, the channels of the hypocaust became filled with material, probably washed in as a result of the space becoming open to the elements, perhaps as the roof decayed. Over this was a layer of rubble, possibly the result either of the demolition of the wing or its collapse. At the northern end of the gallery excavation recovered a pit containing burnt grains of barley and emmer wheat, as well as weed seeds from their cultivation. This shows that cereal crops were still being brought into and processed at the villa even this late in its life. It may be that here we have evidence, paralleled at other villas in southern Britain, that the villa survived as an agricultural centre even if the glory had departed. This would accord well with the fragmentary information from the areas cleared in the 1860s, and discussed above, for sporadic occupation and use late in the life of the villa, but on a much more day-to-day level; and the presence of the millstone in Room 30 slots in with the idea that the former luxury areas had been turned over to agricultural processing.

Quite what the date was when all this occurred is very difficult to establish. The latest coins from Chedworth were minted between 388 and 402, but we do not know how long they circulated before they were lost, deposited or thrown away. It could have been close to their minting date, right at the turn of the fourth and fifth centuries, or it could have been some time thereafter. This is a reflection of the situation across Roman Britain. The latest bronze coins to be supplied to the island from the imperial mints on the Continent are of this 388–402 issue; the number to reach Britain from later mintings of bronze can be counted on the fingers of two hands, so again Chedworth was not behaving unusually. The situation was essentially the same for gold and silver issues, but because of their intrinsic value they are seldom found on occupation sites so are not much use for dating purposes. This cessation of supply is important both for understanding what was happening at the time and for its consequences for modern archaeologists. As argued in the previous chapter, coins were minted by the Roman state in order to discharge its financial obligations, of which the single largest was paying the army, followed by items such as paying the civil service and other imperial projects. For the Roman state to cease supplying coins to Britain meant that it no longer would or could discharge these obligations. Equally, coins in gold, silver and bronze were central to Roman tax-gathering, so the cessation of supply would seem to indicate that the state was no longer raising taxes in Britain. No more eloquent testimony to Britain's slipping out of the Roman Empire could be devised.

Given, as also argued in the previous chapter, that coin was used for such things as commercial transactions, the drying-up of supply must have had serious consequences. There is some evidence for the local counterfeiting of the latest imperial issues to replace the lost official supplies, but this probably did not last long into the fifth century, after which it appears that this commercial economy ceased to operate. If the construction and maintenance of a villa such as Chedworth depended in important part on its being able to dispose of its surplus, so as to pay for goods and services including luxuries such as mosaics, then the collapse of this commercial economy would have impacted seriously on it. In such a scenario one can see how instead of the great luxury residence of the fourth century, there was a move towards a much simpler and more local scale of activity, of the sort suggested above. As well as these changes reflecting growing political instability and economic collapse, what we may also be seeing is a rejection of the high, Roman-style, aristocratic culture that had created and decorated villas such as Chedworth, and the move towards other forms of expression of status, probably much more closely allied to the martial values of a society where increasingly it was military might that mattered.

For archaeologists, the problem is that we lose our most common and reliable dating medium when coins cease to be supplied to Britain. Even more common, of course, was pottery, but that is not intrinsically datable in the way that coins are (except by expensive physical techniques); different types of pottery are actually dated by being found in association with coins of different minting dates. Once the coins stop changing then the pottery can no longer be dated. In fact, it looks as though the mass-produced and widespread pottery of fourth-century Britain did not long outlast the coinage, if at all. This may in part be because we date the pottery by the coins, so they will inevitably seem to 'end' together. Another feature of Roman pottery in Britain was that its shapes and decorative schemes changed over time, yet right at the end this sequence of change stopped, making it probably the last pottery mass-produced in Britain. Its manufacture and distribution most likely depended on the long-distance commercial networks made possible by Roman rule and security, as well as the commercialised economy, and it may have been one of the commodities bought and paid for with coins. Its disappearance might be yet another consequence and also a measure of the disruptions at the end of Roman Britain.

All in all, Chedworth does operate as a sort of microcosm of the 'decline and fall' of Roman Britain. From the bits of evidence we can piece together, it would seem that by the later fourth century the former high standards of decoration and care were starting to slip. What this meant in terms of the household that lived in the villa and what they did is at present impossible to tell. The turning point came somewhere in the first half of the fifth century, probably nearer 400 than 450, with the collapse not only of Roman rule and military presence on the island, but the collapse also of the Roman-style economy and the aristocratic culture that it had supported. This may have taken some time, maybe a generation, as the descendants of the owners of Chedworth struggled to keep up standards; however, in the long run it was a futile attempt. The likelihood is that the grand reception areas and apartments of the villa became simply a series of spaces in which different functions could be performed, largely related to agriculture. The high culture and its appurtenances such as mosaics were a thing of the past. Who the people living in and using these spaces were is a matter for conjecture. Were they the descendants of the old aristocracy, fallen on very hard times? Or had these people abandoned the villa as it became unsustainable, leaving it to the agricultural workers on whose labours the villa had always depended and who now moved into its rooms and galleries? In due course, even they seem to have given up living in the villa and its final and irrevocable decay began.

ABANDONMENT & AFTER

Once the will and the means to maintain the complex buildings of the villa disappeared, the end would come swiftly. The fabric of the buildings would start to decay, through not being maintained, and eventually they would cease to be weatherproof and rain would get in and frost and thaw begin to eat away at the stonework, the wall plaster and the mosaics. The crucial turning point would come once the roofs fell in and the whole structure was open to the weather: it would be only a matter of years before the buildings fell into ruin, as seen so often in the modern world. What we cannot at present tell is whether the buildings were just left to rot or whether there was any element of stripping them of reusable material or purposeful demolition, possibly with the recovery of usable stone. Neither the Victorian nor the more recent excavations seem to have yielded much in the way of structural metalwork, or indeed much metal at all, so it may be that this was recovered. Mention was made above of the large mass of melted lead found in Room 27, possibly a product of just such recovery. Otherwise, there is little evidence for demolition; rather the evidence seems to be for the progressive collapse of buildings as rain penetrated the unprotected walls and frost and thaw forced them apart, and as vegetation in the form of trees and bushes gradually took hold with their roots also forcing the stonework apart.

Another effect of the vegetation would have been to form soil in and around the ruins as the annual shedding of leaves from the trees and bushes, and the dying back of ground-cover plants, provided organic matter. Some of the inorganic material for the soil may have come from the stonework of the villa as it fragmented and pulverised, yielding fine- and coarse-grained detritus. More important in the long run would have been the material washed down the slopes of the valley in which the villa stood by rain, as the measures taken by the builders to prevent this failed – for instance the wall upslope of the north wing and the drain along the back of the wing. This material would have gradually accumulated and, over a long period of time, buried the floors and other surfaces of the villa to a considerable depth, reaching some distance up the stubs of the remaining walls and in turn protecting them against the ravages of the climate. This colluvium is consistently recognised in all excavations at the villa from the Victorians onwards, and accounts for why some walls, especially those nearest the hill-slopes, have survived to some height.

The mixture of detritus from the villa, colluvium and vegetable matter would have been worked and sorted over time by another humble but cumulatively powerful agency: the earthworm. Indeed, Chedworth villa has a walk-on part in Charles Darwin's last publication, *The Formation of Vegetable Mould through the Action of Worms with Observations on their Habits*, published in 1882. The great naturalist was interested in the part earthworms played in creating the soils that buried or part-buried ancient sites, including Stonehenge. In 1877 he sent his sons Francis and Horace to examine the remains at Chedworth, but the thorough clearance of the site thirteen years previously meant there was little left for them to observe. Nevertheless, there was enough to provide satisfactory evidence of the role of earthworms in working the colluvium and organic material, leading to parts of the villa being covered up to a depth of 1m (3ft).

Despite the collapse of roofing and other material on to the floors of the rooms, and despite the protection of some of the walls by colluvium, vegetation and the action of worms, any modern visitor to the site will appreciate that there is a lot more of the villa that has disappeared than remains. How did this come about? The simple answer is that the ruins of a Roman villa provided a ready-made source of cut and shaped building stone – so much less effort than quarrying and shaping fresh supplies. After the end of the Roman period, the next time at which there was a significant demand for building stone was when parish churches started to be built across the countryside, especially in the 300 years or so centring on AD 1000. Reused Roman stone and tile has been recognised in a number of medieval churches near Roman towns or villas, and indeed at Hadrian's Wall and its forts. In the Cotswolds such evidence is hard to come by since the wealth of the region in the later Middle Ages and the availability of excellent freestones has meant that most churches were later extensively reconstructed, hiding their earlier structures. However, were we able to excavate under churches such as Chedworth, Compton Abdale, Withington, Yanworth and perhaps others, it might well be that in the foundations of their earliest phases we would find stones of sizes and shapes showing that they came from a Roman building such as Chedworth. It is impossible to prove from the evidence at Chedworth that this happened. Indeed, if it did it looks as though it was sporadic rather than systematic.

Systematic use of a Roman ruin as a quarry leads to what archaeologists call 'robbing', the removal not just of loose stone on the ground surface or of the upper parts of wall stumps, but of the entire structure down to and including the foundations, leaving 'robber-trenches', the trenches where the foundations had been removed and were just backfilled with earth and/or rejected stone. No trace of this has been observed at Chedworth, so it looks as though, had there been any removal of stone in the Middle Ages, it was not thoroughgoing.

There is evidence that the villa was known about and used as a source of stone later on, probably from the seventeenth century. Up the hill-slope behind the western part of the north wing of the villa was a limekiln, still marked on the earliest editions of the Ordnance Survey map in the earlier part of the nineteenth century. In a limekiln, material such as limestone containing calcium carbonate was burnt to a temperature above 825°C, the process resulting in quicklime, a caustic substance which, when slaked with water and with an aggregate such as sand added, yielded mortar for building. Clearly, the walls of the villa were an easily accessible source of limestone, so this may be where much of the upper parts of the villa have disappeared to. The kiln is not near any village or grand house where the lime might have been used, but presumably it was there because of the source of stone, with the lime it

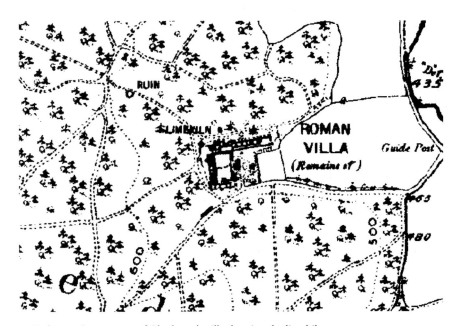

56. Ordnance Survey map of Chedworth villa showing the limekiln.

produced being carted to any building project in the vicinity. Moreover, lime-kiln apart, it is clear that even before the uncovering of the villa in 1864 the site was known about by local people: we have a letter of 1863 by a William Plumb (of whom little is known other than that he was not of the gentry or noble classes so was probably a local man, and literate) relating that the wood-men frequently found Roman remains and material in Chedworth Woods.

JAMES FARRER & THE UNCOVERING OF THE VILLA

The 'discovery' of the villa is traditionally ascribed to the year 1864, a tradi-tion created by the excavator of the villa, James Farrer, according to whom 'The discovery of the Roman villa in these woods originated with an under gamekeeper, engaged in ferreting rabbits, and was first brought under my notice in June 1864'. James Farrer (1812–79) was a man of consequence, three times elected as a Conservative Member of Parliament for South Durham, in 1847–52 and 1852–57 and again from 1859–65, and whose family seat was at Ingleborough near Clapham, in what was then the West Riding of Yorkshire, now part of North Yorkshire. He had already shown considerable inter-est in excavating ancient sites, both near his home, with excavations in the Dowkerbottom caves in 1857 and 1863, and also further afield in the Orkneys, including the famous Neolithic tomb at Maes Howe, in the 1850s. His con-nection with Chedworth was that he acted as guardian to his nephew John Scott, 3rd Lord Eldon (1845–1926). At the time Eldon was legally a minor, so Farrer had oversight on behalf of the trustees of Eldon's estates, centring on Stowell Park between Fossebridge and Northleach, and which included Chedworth Woods.

It seems that Farrer came down to Gloucestershire from time to time, and on one occasion was appraised of Roman remains in the woods, which clearly piqued his antiquarian interests. Unfortunately, we have hardly any detail about the excavations and subsequent works at the site. To judge by Farrer's only published account of the site, appearing the following year in the *Proceedings of the Society of Antiquaries of Scotland*, Vol. VI, he worked very fast, writing in 1865, 'Up to the present time the area of ground already explored is about 2¼ acres', suggesting that pretty much all the site now visible had been cleared in one season of work in 1864. This corresponds with a manuscript account compiled by the long-time resident curator of the site, Norman Irvine, using an account prepared by Fred Norman, one of the workmen who had been employed to uncover the villa. The gamekeeper was one Thomas Margetts, who in what must have been the winter of 1863–64 was acting as loader to Farrer on a shoot and showed him some of the small, squared stones which he had found in the woods, presumably with the help of the aforementioned ferret, and which he had been told were Roman. Farrer recognised these as tesserae from a Roman mosaic and organised some work on the site the following summer.

On the first day they started by uncovering hypocaust channels and fragments of mosaic in what must have been Room 32 at the east end of the north wing. Later in the day the estate steward, Mr Thomas Joachim, paid a visit and remarked that he knew of a visible wall further up in the woods. Workmen sent there to dig a trench soon came down on to a fine mosaic, which proved to be that in the Room 5 *triclinium*. This so enthused Farrer that he collected a much larger team of workers, up to fifty men, and set them to cutting down trees, digging out their roots, finding walls and clearing down into the rooms until some sort of floor or surface was encountered. Soon, what we see of the villa today had been cleared. The techniques used were of their time, workmen armed with picks and shovels clearing away the overburden, the collapse debris of the Roman buildings and the relatively insubstantial remains of the latest occupation in order to uncover the mosaics and other floors. In this way huge amounts of information on the later phases of the villa's life were

57. Farrer's cover buildings. (*National Trust*)

58. Farrer's purpose-built museum. (*National Trust*)

simply shovelled up and thrown away; a matter of huge regret to the modern archaeologist. At the time, however, the existence of such deposits and how to excavate them were not appreciated.

Also in a manner typical of the time, once a mosaic, hypocaust or floor had been discovered, the men stopped. Farrer did not seek to explore and understand any earlier phases of the villa, either. The rapid uncovering of a Roman villa, with its mosaics, baths, hypocausts and interesting objects, by landowners and other gentlemen or clergymen of an antiquarian bent was not uncommon in the middle of the nineteenth century. What makes Chedworth exceptional was what happened next: rather than the remains being reburied (perhaps after the lifting of the more complete mosaics), they were to be preserved, the more spectacular parts covered for protection and a small museum created on the site.

Sadly, either when the Eldon family sold the Stowell Park estate in 1923 or at some later date, all the documentation about the Chedworth Roman villa was either transferred to the new owners and/or was lost or disposed of, so we are in the dark about what happened when and who the prime movers were. In his account of the villa published in 1865, Farrer says that the mosaics and the more important rooms and walls were being preserved, and that the more interesting finds were to be 'deposited in the Museum now building in the woods'. Clearly, therefore, Farrer had taken the initiative in constructing the timber buildings to cover Room 5 with its mosaic, the bathhouse at the end of the west range and Room 23 in the north wing. This in itself was unusual; even more unusual was the idea of building a museum actually on the site to house the finds and display them, rather than removing them to Stowell Park. This seems to have been a personal initiative of Farrer's and marks him out as an innovator in the preservation and display of archaeological sites.

The museum is still there, though now with the shooting lodge attached to its southern side, and is still used for its original purpose, even though its furnishings have considerably altered over time. The earliest arrangement consisted of a sloping, glass-topped case along the south wall, opposite the door, and a long table down the middle of the room. In the case were objects numbered 1–127, with a number of large stone and other objects on the table, taking the numbering up to 157. A catalogue of the objects was prepared by Professor Buckman, who had also worked on Roman remains in Cirencester, and was published in 1872, by which time the museum must have been in operation. Any Roman walls left exposed to the weather would, of course, risk suffering precisely the same destruction as their upper parts had undergone 1,300 years earlier, thanks to rain, frost and thaw, so measures had to be taken to cap the walls to protect them. Farrer seems to have adopted two solutions. The first, and far more effective, was to cap the walls with small roofs made of the hexagonal stone roofing tiles recovered from the Roman debris. These shed the water to each side and prevented the frost damaging the walls beneath. These roofs were certainly picturesque, but they could be slightly confusing given that we normally expect roofs to cover a building, not a wall. Much less satisfactory was simply topping the walls with horizontal slabs of limestone brought into the site; this method did not waterproof the walls, with the consequence that frost and thaw led them to shatter. What had not been appreciated until recently was the extent to which the Roman walls were rebuilt or heightened at this date, meaning that much of what is currently on display is in fact a nineteenth-century version of a Roman villa, albeit with reused fallen Roman masonry for the facing stones. Some of these walls do not precisely follow the lines of their Roman predecessors, though with the exception of part of the southern half of the cross-gallery this is a minor difference. This capping had certainly been done by 1869 when it is mentioned by a Mr Marshall in his account of a visit to the site.

When James Farrer ceased to be involved with the Chedworth villa after the rupture with Lord Eldon in 1886 (see below), one of the adverse

59. Farrer's method of capping the walls. (*National Trust*)

consequences was that he never published any substantial account of what he found, apart from his piece in the *Proceedings of the Society of Antiquaries of Scotland*; this is an enormous loss to our knowledge of the site. Also, the observations he recorded at the time and any records in the Stowell estate archives have not survived the passage of time. There was some supplementary publication on the site, provoked largely by the presence of the chi-rhos on the *nymphaeum* coping stones and thus clear evidence for Roman-period Christianity. There was little evidence available in the nineteenth century for Christianity in Roman Britain, so any new evidence was of great interest in what was then still a Christian and church- or chapel-going country.

One of the early visitors to the work on the villa was Revd Samuel Lysons, son of the noted antiquary responsible for uncovering the great villas at Bignor (West Sussex) and Woodchester (Gloucestershire) at the turn of the eighteenth and nineteenth centuries. As a clergyman, his interest was principally in the evidence for Christianity, which he published in Volume 4 of the *Cotteswold Naturalists Field Club* (1867); in this he set running a couple of entertaining hares in noting the inscription from the villa which he read as PRASYTA and linked with the name Prasutagus, and also the presence nearby of Roman bricks stamped ARVIRI, which he associated with the mythical character Arvirargus. He also discussed his ideas with other antiquaries, one of whom was J.W. Grover, who published in the 1867 volume of the *Journal of the British Archaeological Association* (Vol. 23) a discussion of the evidence for Christianity in Britain before the mission of St Augustine of Canterbury (from 597), citing the evidence from Chedworth and Lysons' views on it. In the following year he published an account of the Chedworth villa in the *Journal of the British Archaeological Association* (Vol. 24). In both these articles Grover developed Lysons' ideas on the matter of Arvirargus and Prasutagus. He noted the inscribed stone from the villa which he read as PRASIATA (see p. 102 for the current explanation of this) and thus referring to Prasutagus, husband of Boadicea, whose death set in train the events which led to the great revolt against Rome in 61 led by the vengeful queen.

Grover also noted that earlier excavations on the site of a Roman bathhouse at Listercombe Bottom, not far from Chedworth, had yielded a number of tiles stamped ARVIRI (modern scholarship reads them as ARVERI). He took this as evidence of the Briton named Arvirargus, mentioned by the Roman poet Juvenal (*Satire* 4) at the turn of the first and second centuries but otherwise utterly unknown. Arvirargus, however, recurs as a figure in the mythical history of Geoffrey of Monmouth writing in the early twelfth century, where he is presented as the son of Kimbelinus, fighting against the Roman Emperor Claudius when the latter invaded Britain in 43. Arvirargus does indeed appear as a minor part in Shakespeare's *Cymbeline*. Grover goes on to cite unnamed 'old chroniclers' to conclude that Arvirargus was the father of Boadicea and that he was converted to Christianity by Joseph of Arimathea (more usually associated in legend with Glastonbury), thus proving to his own satisfaction that Chedworth villa was associated with these personages. His discussion culminates, '... and it is, perhaps, not too much to say that these pavements have been trodden by the royal feet of Boadicea'. Later in the article he even manages to associate a number of incised Xs on stones at Chedworth and in the vicinity with the account of Arvirargus in the fifteenth-century verse of chronicler John Hardyng, and the adoption of the Cross of St George and thus the origins of the Union flag. Examples, one may reasonably think, of misplaced ingenuity.

Another interested clerical antiquary was Revd H.M. Scarth, who guided the visit of the British Archaeological Association to the site during its Cirencester congress in 1868 and subsequently presented his version in the *Journal of the British Archaeological Association* for the following year. He largely based this on Farrer's account, picking up Grover's ideas on Arvirargus and Prasutagus from the previous year's journal, but being markedly more circumspect. This article and the account of the Association's visit to Chedworth elicited James Farrer's only other published writings on the villa. In a letter

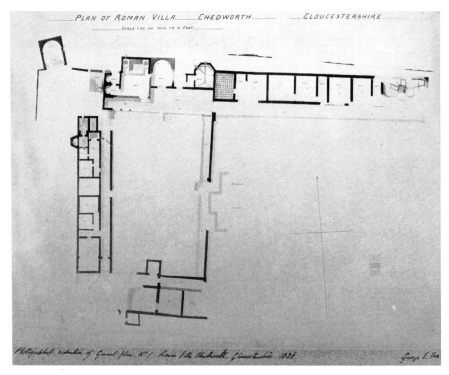

60. Plan of the villa by G.E. Fox. (*David Woods / The Society of Antiquaries of London*)

dated 5 February and published in the volume of the *Journal* for that year, Farrer supplied Scarth with further and better particulars of the emptying of the pool of the *nymphaeum* and of the condition of that structure as revealed.

The last substantial paper on the Chedworth villa was published in the 1887 volume (Vol. 44) of the *Archaeological Journal* by G.E. Fox (who is utterly silent on Arvirargus and Prasutagus). In it he proposed a theory which was to hold sway for three-quarters of a century. He was not convinced that what Farrer had interpreted as a set of baths at the west end of the north wing was actually a bathhouse, since he did not believe that what were presented as plunge baths were actually such amenities. He preferred to see this whole group of rooms as a cloth-finishing establishment, a *fullonica*. In this he was clearly influenced by the descriptions of the *fullonicae* at Pompeii, interpreting the Chedworth 'tanks', as he called them, as the places where the cloth was trodden with cleaning agents. He pointed out that there were exposures of Fullers Earth in the sides of the Chedworth combe, Fullers Earth being a fine clay which when mixed with water and applied to cloth, particularly woollen cloth, removed lanolin, greases and dirt. Apart from this departure, he was, as were the other writers mentioned above, dependent on the publication of Farrer in 1865, as well as visits to the site and museum (Fox produced some very elegant drawings of some of the stonework from the villa). Therefore, although these articles advanced new hypotheses and interpretations, of varying plausibility, none of them increased our knowledge of what had actually been discovered at the site beyond what Farrer had reported.

One other Roman structure was uncovered as part of Farrer's investigations in Chedworth Woods: part of a building to the north-west of the villa, which he named The Capitol (discussed in the previous chapter). This site has a later history that is worth the telling. By the time of the uncovering of the villa in 1864, this part of the woods was already under another threat. In 1861 a meeting had been held to propose a railway line along the Coln valley linking Cheltenham through to Lechlade and beyond. In the event this plan came to nothing. However, some thirty years later a version of this project did come to pass with the construction of the Midland and South Western Junction Railway.

This was incorporated in 1881 and the line from Swindon to Cirencester constructed. The line of the planned continuation of the route took the railway very close to the western side of the Chedworth villa. Lord Eldon was bitterly opposed to the construction of the line since it would slice through his estates, and secured modifications to the 1884 Act of Parliament re-incorporating the Midland and South Western Junction Railway, which

61. A railway engine at the cutting at Chedworth. (*National Trust*)

among other things required the proposed route to be moved further to the west and that there should be 'the minimum of interference with archaeo-logical objects ... and that all such objects ... shall remain ... the property of the said Earl of Eldon'. It is interesting that Lord Eldon was that much exercised about the villa and the surrounding archaeology. Once the line was built, it is said that Lord Eldon took care never to travel on it himself and forbade estate produce to be moved on it or for goods for the estate to be delivered on it. The line had stations at Chedworth village and Withington, which made visiting the villa much easier. Despite the provisions of the 1884 Act, the construction of the line in 1889–90 badly damaged The Capitol, and its reconstruction and widening in 1901–02 finally obliterated it.

LORD ELDON & THE VILLA DISPLAYED

Let us return to Lord Eldon (see colour plate 27). In 1866 Lord Eldon attained the age of 21 and his majority; he thus came into the control of his estates. He and his guardian, James Farrer, seem to have parted ways soon afterwards and not on the best of terms, though unfortunately we do not know what the rea-sons for this were; maybe it was simply that the young Lord Eldon wished to manage his own affairs. An account of the visit of the British Archaeological Association to the villa in 1868 states that Farrer was intending to pursue his investigations in the woods once the leaves were off, but this is the last men-tion we have of him in connection with the site. There is no evidence he was actually present for the visit and his intention seems to have been unrealised. Nevertheless, it is clear that Eldon was interested by the remains Farrer had uncovered; for one thing he did not order them to be simply reburied. On the contrary, he made them a feature of his estate and the social life and activities on it. This was done by building on to Farrer's on-site museum a very con-siderable extension to house a shooting lodge, in which his guests could be entertained by the Roman structures which formed an unusual and remark-able edging to the grounds of the lodge.

The lodge was constructed on the spoil removed in uncovering the villa; this had largely been thrown downslope to the east of the Roman cross-gallery, thus obscuring the form of the western part of the lower courtyard of the villa and covering the approach to the cross-gallery and the entrance to the garden court. The building itself was constructed of local stone for the ground floor, the upper floor being of a timber-framed construction with brick infilling.

62. The shooting lodge in the 1870s. (*Society of Antiquaries of London*)

On the ground floor were two large rooms: one for the entertaining of important guests, still retaining a very fine chimneypiece decorated with the arms of the Scott (Eldon) family; the other a simpler room for less honoured members of the party. In front (east) of the main door of the lodge was a large turning circle for carriages; on its eastern side was a large, octagonal garden feature, which also acted as a vantage point with a panoramic view over the lower part of the combe in which the villa lies, the Coln and the landscape beyond. The lodge seems to have been built in 1867 and photographs of 1870 or a bit later show it newly built.

The lodge was approached by the new access road that had been created along the southern side of the valley, still in operation today. Aerial views of the site taken in the 1940s, when the entrance to the villa was still past the lodge, and before the turning circle and the garden feature had been allowed to degrade, show how very different the relationship of the Roman villa and the nineteenth-century buildings was then to that of today. Now the museum and lodge are subordinate to the Roman structures, if not actually intrusive into them, whereas in the late nineteenth and early twentieth centuries it was the remains of the villa that were adjunct to the shooting lodge. The focus of the ensemble was clearly the lodge/museum building set in its grounds with parterres and specimen trees to the front and rear. The upstanding walls of the

63. The fireplace in the shooting lodge. (*National Trust*)

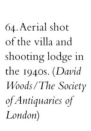

64. Aerial shot of the villa and shooting lodge in the 1940s. (*David Woods / The Society of Antiquaries of London*)

villa and the cover-buildings over parts of the west range and the north wing essentially formed a backdrop, and shooting-party guests were presumably given a guided tour or allowed to wander at will to marvel at Lord Eldon's unique conversation-piece antiquities.

The lodge's period of use for its original purpose may not have lasted much above a decade, as in the mid-1880s what was then the head keeper's cottage at Yanworth mill was extended, including a room suitable for entertaining shooting parties. Given the importance that Lord Eldon's fourth-century predecessors in the valley accorded to hunting, it is pleasing that in the nineteenth century their villa was again the setting for a similar activity, even if Lord Eldon did not realise the connection. It is a pity that we cannot now know how Lord Eldon, an aristocrat educated in the Greek and Roman classics at Eton and Christ Church, Oxford, a Cotswold landowner, leading member of local society, and a regular huntsman, saw his Romano-British predecessors: he might have found them more familiar than he would have thought.

We know very little about either the number or the type of visitors to the villa during the later nineteenth century and early twentieth century when the site remained in the possession of the Scott family and formed part of the Stowell estate. Obviously, there would have been the aristocratic and other important guests who made up the Stowell Park shooting parties, but unfortunately no records of these have survived; nor do we have any accounts of the impression the site made on them. That other visitors to the villa were envisaged from early on is attested by the publication in 1872 of the first guidebook, prepared by Professor Buckman and Mr R. W. Hall, and containing a catalogue of the objects on display in the museum. This was printed by a Cirencester firm and sold for 6d, therefore it was clearly viewed as a commercial proposition rather than simply a souvenir guide for the earl's guests. Access to the site was made easier by the construction of the railway in 1889–90 with its stations at Chedworth village and Withington; indeed, special reduced-rate tickets to Chedworth station from the principal stations on the line were sold – the fact that admission to the site was free would have helped.

From the start of the twentieth century access to the villa by car or by charabanc would have become an increasingly practical consideration. Clearly, the villa did become a more popular destination for visitors in the Edwardian period, as may be judged by the increasing numbers of postcards of the site being produced for sale, with some printings running into the thousands. As early as 1867 the members of the newly founded Cotteswold Naturalists Field Club used their first field visit to inspect the remains of the villa, as recorded in Volume 4 of their journal, along with the observations of Revd Lysons mentioned above. Then there was the British Archaeological Association's visit in 1868, also mentioned above. Another group of visitors of which we have a record included members of the Bristol and Gloucestershire Archaeological Society, whose visit to the villa on 18 July 1889 was immortalised in a photograph; this showed the group posing in the angle between the west range and the north wing with the museum and shooting lodge as a backdrop. Hardly any of the villa is visible giving an idea of the state of the remains, though the presence of a marquee over the southern half of the garden court may suggest the Society was well looked after on its visit.

Not all visitors were so high-minded. For them creature comforts and entertainment were taken care of by Mr Hoare, who had become the tenant of the lodge. Along with his nephew Marty, he sold bottles of lemonade and ginger beer to the visitors and arranged for a fire setting outside the south-western angle of the villa so visitors could have a 'brew–up'. Even less archaeological was the turning over of the space outside the colonnade of the north baths (Room 20) to be a skittle alley, with glass bottles as the skittles, these being rediscovered in the excavations of the 1960s. On the plus side, Mr Hoare was an enthusiastic gardener and seems to have had further borders laid out around the lodge and also a new vegetable garden in the field down

65. The visit of the Bristol and Gloucestershire Archaeological Society. (*Gloucestershire Archives*)

66. Postcard of the villa in the early twentieth century. (*National Trust*)

below the eastern side of the lodge in the lower part of the combe; postcards of the time show the lawns and flowerbeds immaculately tended.

If the gardens attached to the lodge were well kept, there is less certainty about the state of the villa remains themselves. Photographs of around 1895, particularly along the north wing, show the remains well cared for and the grass kept short, though trees had been allowed to grow in Room 27 and probably Rooms 28 and 29: their roots will have damaged any remaining archaeology. Other photographs of about 1901 confirm this impression, though there is a slightly unkempt air as plants were establishing themselves in the walls, and trees and bushes were coming close to the back wall of the north wing. Postcards dating to the later 1920s, however, show the villa still well maintained with much of the grass kept mown (unless this was for the benefit of the photographer) and the walls and their coverings in a good state of repair.

ST CLAIR BADDELEY & THE NATIONAL TRUST

After the First World War, Stowell seems to have been passing through hard times, and Lord Eldon decided to sell the estate to retrench and concentrate on the family's main seat at Encombe in Dorset. The first attempt at auction in 1923 was not successful and the estate was reoffered for sale the following year. By then the attention had been attracted of the sonorously named Welbore St Clair Baddeley – traveller, dramatist, poet and antiquary – of Castle Hale, Painswick, in the county of Gloucestershire. He determined that the villa, museum and shooting lodge and their immediate surroundings should be purchased by public subscription from the estate, preserved and opened for the public good. After an inauspicious start, the project received the support of *The Times* newspaper and the £2,500 asking price was finally achieved at a meeting of the Bristol and Gloucestershire Archaeological Society at its meeting at Stow-on-the-Wold; here, a Bristol solicitor stumped up £100 and a whip-round was organised to secure the last £95 or so needed. By this time it had been determined that the best destination for the villa was the National Trust, though no papers survive to suggest how this was negotiated and why the Trust was willing to accept a property markedly different from those

which constituted its then rapidly increasing portfolio of country houses and the like.

Once the transfer of the site to the National Trust had been effected, St Clair Baddeley took a further interest, excavating on the site of the Roman temple or mausoleum to the south-east of the villa (see previous chapter, p. 126), which he published in Vol. 52 (1930) of the *Transactions of the Bristol and Gloucestershire*

67. Welbore St Clair Baddeley. (*National Trust*)

Archaeological Society. By coincidence, a report to the Trust on visitor numbers for that year survives, showing a grand total of 6,071 persons, among them members of the British Association for the Advancement of Science and a number of school parties, mainly from Gloucestershire. For a time when car ownership was not yet widespread, this seems a respectable number of visitors to an out-of-the-way site. With the transfer to the National Trust came the imposition for the first time of an entrance fee, apparently 1*s*. In order to improve the visitors' experience, St Clair Baddeley prepared the first new guidebook for the site in some sixty years, the first edition of which was published in 1925 at a price of 9*d*. A second edition was published in 1928 with extra content, but the price increased to 1*s*. With the transfer, the Trust also gained the sitting tenant of the shooting lodge, a Mrs Irvine and her son Norman, who apart from service in the Second World War was to remain at the villa for most of his life, serving as resident custodian until 1977, and awarded the British Empire Medal in 1974.

After this burst of activity, the site seems to have returned to a rather sleepy state in the 1930s. The war years saw the departure of Norman Irvine and the

68. Norman Irvine. (*National Trust*)

site was essentially put into cold storage for the duration. Once the war was over, the Trust was remarkably quick off the mark in making provision for its reopening, for the repair of damage suffered due to the neglect during the war and for considering the future of the site. A report of the present condition of the site and the works needed was commissioned from Sir Cyril Fox, Director of the National Museum of Wales; he made the report in December 1945 and, apart from identifying practical works, recommended the production of a new guidebook as visitors started to return.

All this was put in hand, and letters survive from James Lees-Milne, at the time secretary to the Historic Buildings Committee of the Trust (formerly the Country Houses Committee, a revealing title), recording visits to Chedworth and progress on the restoration; an updated version of the guidebook appeared over the initials JL-M in 1949. In addition, a complete re-equipping of the museum was undertaken on the advice of the Ashmolean Museum, Oxford, with new cases and storage acquired so the collection could be afforded a new display and the material not on display could be safely stored; at the same time the exterior of the shooting lodge was repaired and repainted. The programme of works and Lees-Milne's visits to the sites ignited what was to be a long-running debate after the war, since some of the Victorian wall-cappings were showing their age. The question was what to do about protecting the wall-tops and which of the various alternatives would be both practical and aesthetically pleasing. Related to this was the developing debate over whether to use cement or a lime mortar where walls needed rebuilding or repointing.

Excavation resumed in 1954 when Eve Rutter re-excavated Room 4, which until then had been known as the 'porter's lodge', on no very good grounds. Her work showed that it was in fact a latrine attached to the south side of the south wing. In the aftermath of this work, another major figure in the history of the villa under the National Trust became involved: (Sir) Ian Richmond, first Professor of the Archaeology of the Roman Provinces in the University of Oxford. In the 1959 Volume (78) of the *Transactions of the Bristol and Gloucestershire Archaeological Society*, Richmond published a discussion of the villa, in which he laid down the modern understanding of its development from three simple, second-century buildings to the grand, fourth-century residence with its three wings linked by galleries, its two bathhouses and floored with a number of mosaics and other architectural embellishments. In so doing, he contradicted Fox's argument that the installations at the west end of the north wing were for cloth-finishing and restored them to their proper function as a set of baths. Late in the same year he supplied the National Trust with a five-year plan for conservation and

69. Sir Ian Richmond and the workmen at the Chedworth villa. (*National Trust*)

further research at the villa; he also proposed a new cover-building for the North Wing baths, as well as the production of a new guidebook.

Between the late 1950s and 1964 Richmond undertook a series of excavations, above all on the north baths in which he disentangled the complex structural sequence in that area. His sudden death in 1965 meant that the results of this work were not brought to full publication, a situation exacerbated by the fact that he kept little in the way of excavation records. He did, nevertheless, address the Royal Archaeological Institute when it visited the site during its summer meeting in 1964 and this talk was published in the following year's volume (122) of the *Archaeological Journal*, repeating his views on the overall sequence but adding quite definite dates for which he could not give the full details in such a short summary. Richmond's contribution to our knowledge and understanding of the villa through unravelling the sequence of the north baths was considerable; so also was the annoyance his restorations of parts of the building provoked at the National Trust. Without consulting with the Trust, which by then had clear views on the conservation of the fabric of historic buildings, he capped some of the walls with little roofs, rather in the manner of Farrer's capping, but using mechanically produced tiles; other walls he capped with pre-cast concrete slabs. The lines of the walls in the north baths that he had excavated then reburied were marked with reddish concrete between concrete kerbing slabs. In internal National Trust correspondence this all attracted words such as 'appalling' and 'ugly', one letter describing Richmond as 'an extremely prickly don'; however, his death closed down the discussion on how to get him 'to cease his concrete practices'.

70. Richmond's restoration of the walls and wall-tops. (*National Trust*)

A small excavation was needed on the outside of the south-western angle of the villa in 1977, in advance of the construction of the new visitor centre; it revealed a wall running west from the angle, continuing the line of the south wall of the south wing and presumably acting as a boundary wall for the area to the west of the west range. That year the Oxford connection was resumed with Roger Goodburn, research assistant to Richmond's successor, Professor S.S. Frere: he was asked for his advice and involvement, and in the following year he and his collaborator Sally Stow initiated a series of small-scale interventions which would carry through to 1990. These were designed to clarify details of the structural history of the villa, as well as to investigate in advance of conservation works undertaken by the National Trust. In the process they considerably advanced understanding of the west range and the cross-gallery.

In 1972 Goodburn produced an entirely new and updated guidebook to a larger format and well illustrated, replacing the one that had appeared in various forms for half a century and more. In 1981 he also produced an abbreviated version for those who did not want the larger, more expensive book. One of Goodburn's excavations, in 1983, lay just east of the entrance to the shooting lodge and made contact with walls which seemed to be the continuation of the south wing. A larger-scale excavation further down the slope to the east was undertaken by Philip Bethell in 1997 to test whether this was in fact the case. This showed that the south wing did continue through this area with a

71. Roger Goodburn and Sally Stow excavating at Chedworth. (*National Trust*)

layout similar to that elsewhere in the villa of a gallery fronting a range of rooms (see Chapter 2 for a fuller consideration). In the same decade three geophysical surveys were carried out, two of them over the whole area in the possession of the National Trust, though most of what they showed more likely relates to the site since 1864, such as utilities for the shooting lodge and various paths laid as part of the presentation of the villa. At the beginning of the new millennium, excavations were carried out in 2000 and 2001 by Dr Maureen Carroll of the University of Sheffield in the garden court, in order to see whether any features relating to a formal garden layout had survived. In the event, this proved not to be so, although several features relating to the water system of the villa were discovered (see Chapter 2). A geophysical survey associated with this work in the field to the east of the lower part of the villa, Fallfield, was undertaken and showed the approach road to the villa and traces of structures fronting on to it.

By this time it was clear that the cover-buildings erected by Farrer, though several times restored and re-roofed, were approaching the end of their useful life. They were, moreover, cramped and poorly lit, so were not a great asset in explaining the Roman site to visitors. In addition, features of previous conservation work at the villa, such as the little roofs capping many of the walls and the reddish concrete laid by Richmond to mark where walls had stood, were felt to be at the least unhelpful to the visitors' understanding of the remains, if not downright confusing. Furthermore, some of the wall-cappings were showing their age and becoming less protective of what lay beneath them.

The time seemed ripe for a major project of re-presentation of the villa to the public, who now came to the site in considerable numbers, of the order of 65,000 a year, over ten times the number who visited in 1930 in the early years of the National Trust's ownership. Instead of the accretion of small-scale repairs and restorations, there should be a single, far-reaching programme to reinterpret and redisplay the villa in a way that would make it more comprehensible and enable visitors to better understand what the remains represented. In order to accomplish this substantial scheme, funds were needed, over and above what the National Trust could provide out of its own resources. Accordingly, a bid was put in to the Heritage Lottery Fund in 2001 to construct new buildings that would cover the entirety of the west range, as well as the western half of the north wing, along with enhancing the 'visitor experience' by providing better visibility of the remains, new signage and other explanatory media such as an audio-visual guide. This bid was unsuccessful in its initial form, but after consultation with the Heritage Lottery Fund, a revised bid was submitted in 2007, this time seeking only a building to cover the west range; this bid proved successful and work on the building commenced in late 2010. It was completed a year later, ready for a reopening of the site in spring 2012 (see colour plate 28).

One of the striking changes that the bidding process required and demonstrated was in what might be termed the 'target audience' of the villa in the century and a half since its uncovering by James Farrer. In Lord Eldon's day the audience was in part composed of the earl's guests, the aristocratic and the well-to-do; otherwise it was those sufficiently interested to make the trek out to the site. In the late nineteenth and early part of the twentieth centuries, interested visitors were either organised parties from national and local learned societies or individuals with a particular passion for antiquities of the Roman period. Numbers presumably increased with the opening of the branch line late in the nineteenth century. When the site passed into the ownership of the National Trust in 1924, the clientele for visiting the villa seems, to judge from a report of 1930, already to have included a number of school parties. Since the Second World War, the National Trust has been increasingly concerned with diversifying its visitor base. This has always been a feature of Chedworth, since its relative isolation can mean that it is more efficacious to get visitors there in groups than singly. Therefore, it has long been a target for school parties, the more so since the introduction of the National Curriculum; the provision for the study of Roman Britain means the villa can function as a hands-on laboratory for encountering the Roman past.

The Heritage Lottery Fund is very insistent that projects to which its grants are accorded should make every effort to reach out and engage the widest possible community, including those to whom heritage is not a normal (or even abnormal) part of their experience and also those who come from communities whose heritage is not necessarily that of the British Isles. Were Lord Eldon to revisit his villa now in the twenty-first century, among the many things that have changed, perhaps it would be the numbers and the composition of the visiting public that would most surprise him. One other opportunity that was provided by the rise in importance of this property to the National Trust was the decision to try to systematise and publish as much knowledge as could be recovered about the villa in the Roman period and its history since its rediscovery; after all, even after nearly a century and a half there had never been a full, systematic publication and discussion of the site for specialists and non-specialists alike. The provision of the new buildings and displays at Chedworth and the publication of what we know of the villa up to 2011 have, as it were, drawn a line under those first 150 years of its modern history. But there remains much that we would like to know about Chedworth villa and its setting, which will only be achieved by further research and excavation on and around the site.

FURTHER READING

Readers of this book may wish to find out more about the various topics covered. This section contains publications on topics of immediate relevance to the Chedworth villa, such as the nineteenth-century publications on the site, but also more general works concerned with aspects of late Roman Britain or the late Roman world more widely that have been drawn upon to construct the picture given here. Because of the circumstances of the various excavations on the site from 1864 onwards, there has never yet been a full and detailed publication of the villa; such a publication is now in hand and should appear in the next couple of years.

Introduction
Two: The Layout of the Late Roman Villa

James Farrer never produced a major publication on his uncovering of the villa in 1864, presumably as a result of his split with Lord Eldon soon after. The most substantial account he gave is, J. Farrer, 'Notice of recent excavation in Chedworth Wood, on the estate of the Earl of Eldon in the County of Gloucester', *Proceedings of the Society of Antiquaries of Scotland*, Vol. 6, Pt. 2 (1965), pp. 278–83.

The most substantial nineteenth-century publication of the site was that by G.E. Fox, 'The Roman Villa at Chedworth, Gloucestershire', *Archaeological Journal*, Vol. 44 (1887), pp. 322–36, which formed the basis for guidebooks and other publications down into the twentieth century.

Sir Ian Richmond died before he could publish his excavations on the villa in the 1950s, but his developing views are contained in his article, I.A. Richmond, 'The Roman Villa at Chedworth, 1958–59', *Transactions of the Bristol and Gloucestershire Archaeological Society*, Vol. 78 (1959), pp. 5–23.

Roger Goodburn's 1972 National Trust guidebook to the site gave the fullest account to date of the villa and remains of great value: R. Goodburn, *The Roman Villa Chedworth* (originally published 1972, revised and reprinted several times).

The excavations by Roger Goodburn and Sally Stow, along with those by Philip Bethell, Maureen Carroll and others, will be published in the forthcoming monograph, but they have all kindly made their findings available for the writing of this book.

Three: Experiencing the Late Roman Villa

The ways in which a late Roman aristocratic residence was laid out and functioned are discussed in S.P. Ellis, *Roman Housing* (Duckworth, 2000), and for Britain more specifically in D. Perring, *The Roman House in Britain* (Routledge, 2002).

Mosaics are discussed and lavishly illustrated in S. Cosh and D. Neal, *Roman Mosaics of Britain: Volume IV Western Britain* (Society of Antiquaries, London, 2010). The subject matter of Roman mosaics in Britain more generally is reviewed in P. Witts, *Mosaics in Roman Britain: stories in stone* (Tempus, 2005).

M. Henig, *The Art of Roman Britain* (Batsford, 1995), considers the various mediums and meanings of the arts in the Roman period in Britain.

Four: Men, Women and Gods

For a survey of many aspects of the Roman family see B. Rawson (ed.), *A Companion to Families in the Greek and Roman Worlds* (Blackwell, 2010).

For later Roman education, see R.A. Kaster, *Guardians of Language: The Grammarian and Society in Late Antiquity* (University of California Press, 1997).

The traditional religions of Roman Britain are treated by M. Henig, *Religion in Roman Britain* (Batsford, 1984). The arrival of Christianity is discussed in D. Petts, *Christianity in Roman Britain* (Tempus, 2003).

Five: Competitive Entertaining

The activities comprising a Roman hunt and the social significance of hunting are considered in J.K. Anderson, *Hunting in the Ancient World* (University of California Press, 1985).

Baths with bathing and its meaning in the Roman worlds are discussed by F. Yegül, *Bathing in the Roman World* (Cambridge University Press, 2010) and G. Fagan, *Bathing in Public in the Roman World* (Michigan, 1999).

Roman formal dining, its setting, personnel and rituals are laid out in K. Dunbabin, *The Roman Banquet: images of conviviality* (Cambridge University Press, 2003). H.E.M. Cool, *Eating and Drinking in Roman Britain* (Cambridge University Press, 2006) looks at the evidence for Britain more specifically.

Six: The Villa in the Landscape

A general introduction to the Roman period in Gloucestershire is T. Copeland: *Roman Gloucestershire* (The History Press, 2011). A detailed catalogue of Romano-British sites in the Cotswolds is afforded by the volume by the Royal Commission on Historical Monuments (England): *Iron Age and Romano-British Monuments in the Gloucestershire Cotswolds* (HMSO, 1976).

Villa culture in late Roman Britain more widely is presented by G. de la Bédoyère, *The Golden Age of Roman Britain* (Tempus, 1999).

Roman coins and their uses in Britain are clearly presented in R. Reece: *The Coinage of Roman Britain* (Tempus, 2002). For pottery a comprehensive survey is P. Tyers, *Atlas of Roman Pottery in Britain* (Oxbow Books, 2011).

Seven: Oblivion and Rediscovery

For the circumstances surrounding the collapse of Roman rule in Britain, see A.S. Esmonde Cleary, *The Ending of Roman Britain* (Batsford, 1989) and N. Faulkner, *The Decline and Fall of Roman Britain* (Tempus, 2000). Roger White, *Britannia Prima: Britain's Last Roman Province* (Tempus, 2007) looks more specifically at the late Roman period and after in south-western Britain.

INDEX